The Institutional Context of Poverty Eradication in Rural Africa

Proceedings from a Seminar in Tribute to the 20th Anniversary of the International Fund for Agricultural Development (IFAD)

Edited by
Kjell J. Havnevik
with Emil Sandström

Nordiska Afrikainstitutet 2000

This book has been published with financial support from
the Swedish Ministry for Foreign Affairs.

Indexing terms

Poverty alleviations
Rural areas
Conference papers
Africa

Language checking: Elaine Almén
Cover: Alicja Grenberger

ISBN 91-7106-460-5

Printed in Sweden by Elanders Gotab, Stockholm 2000

Contents

Acknowledgements

The idea to undertake this seminar in tribute to IFAD's 20th anniversary originated in the Swedish Foreign Ministry which joined hands with the Nordic Africa Institute and the Department of Rural Development Studies, the Swedish University of Agricultural Sciences, in its planning and subsequent implementation.

In the Foreign Ministry in Stockholm Lennart Båge, Gunilla Olsson, Elisabet Brolin and Pernilla Josefsson contributed to the process in various ways alongside Dorrit Alopaeus-Ståhl, who supported from her base in Rome.

The major part of the planning and implementation of the seminar was carried out by Emil Sandström and Kjell J. Havnevik at the Department of Rural Development Studies, the Swedish University of Agricultural Sciences. Intermittently support for the process was also given by Lennart Wohlgemuth, the Nordic Africa Institute.

During the seminar sessions prepared contributions were also provided by Gloria Davis, the World Bank, Oliver Saasa, the University of Zambia, Jan Cedergren, the Swedish Foreign Ministry, Johan Holmberg, the Swedish International Development Agency, Sida and Atiqur Rahman, IFAD. Most of these, however, only appeared in verbal form and are hence not included in these proceedings.

Work on the seminar proceedings was conducted by Kjell Havnevik who received important contributions from Emil Sandström, and not least from the contributors who willingly submitted their written presentations, some of which were updated and modified to capture the most recent developments related to poverty eradication in Sub-Saharan Africa. For this we are most grateful. Gunilla Olsson, the Swedish Foreign Ministry, also contributed important advice during this last process.

The President of IFAD, Fawzi H. Al-Sultan, and his staff contributed advice and literature of relevance for the planning of the seminar and contributed as well in a most constructive way during the two day venue. An important side event of the seminar itself, was the bringing of the IFAD sponsored exhibition, "From Hope to Harvest", to the Swedish University of Agricultural Sciences in Uppsala, which made available to students and the concerned public in the Uppsala/Stockholm region, important knowledge and ideas related to rural development and poverty alleviation in African rural areas.

Uppsala, November 1999

Kjell J. Havnevik

Chapter 1
Introduction

Kjell J. Havnevik

Seminar objectives

The seminar set out to inquire into what were considered the most critical issues related to African rural poverty generation and eradication, i.e. the institutional context of poverty. The role of institutions for capturing productive benefits for smallholders, for political mobilisation against poverty and for rural people's access to and control over economic, political and social resources was placed in focus. The institutional and organisational issues related to the poverty context have often been overlooked or have been poorly understood by many who are involved and engaged in combating poverty in Africa. In putting these issues on top of the agenda the seminar hoped that a fruitful and constructive discussion could unfold where policy makers, representatives from government and other assistance organisations, activists and researchers would participate and learn from each other.

The seminar further placed the institutional context of poverty within the broader framework of economic and political reforms, which have also been central to rural development in Africa during the last two decades. Economic reforms were initiated in the early 1980s, and political reforms from the beginning of the 1990s. Hence a crucial focus of the seminar came to be an analysis of the changing context of rural development on the ground in rural Africa and how it interrelated with the economic and political reforms.

The seminar did not only put emphasis on past experiences and contemporary trends, but focused as well on the options available for poverty eradication and alleviation in the future. This was done both from the standpoint of the conditions in the rural areas themselves but also based on the potential deriving from new ideas related to development assistance such as the partnership approach.

Background

The poverty context in rural Africa had already been a major concern for the Nordic governments from the onset of the African crisis in the late 1970s. They all tried to identify ways and channels to support soundly based and well informed poverty eradication and poverty alleviation initiatives. In this context the Swedish government made the decision to take an active part in the creation and subsequent support of the International Fund for Agricultural Development, IFAD, which was established in 1978. Two decades later, in 1998, the Swedish government wished to pay tribute to IFAD's long and devoted attention to issues concerning poverty reduction in rural Africa. Such issues ought, according to the Swedish and other Nordic governments, to have been considered issues of prime importance throughout, although, in particular during the 1980s, they were often overlooked or poorly understood by many international institutions and assistance agencies.

The Swedish government joined hands with the Nordic Africa Institute and the Department of Rural Development Studies, the Swedish University of Agricultural Sciences, both of Uppsala, Sweden, in organising a seminar in tribute to IFAD's 20th Anniversary. The title of the seminar was "Issues, Experiences and Options for Eradicating Poverty in Rural Africa". The latter two organising institutions also have a keen interest and commitment not only to research on the institutional context of poverty in rural Africa, but also in relation to how such research can be translated into viable and realistic policies for the future.

Researchers, policy makers and concerned people from Nordic and African government institutions, various non-governmental organisations and institutions such as the World Bank, IFAD, UNRISD, University of Wales Swansea, Oxford University, University of Zambia, Nordic Africa Institute and Swedish University of Agricultural Sciences met for two intensive days of presentations and discussions on the seminar topic.

Since May 1998, the time of the seminar, the issue of African poverty has received increased attention. In late 1999 when Nelson Mandela addressed the Organisation of Trade Union Unity in Johannesburg, he described poverty in Africa as "the number one problem of the world" (Mustapha)[*] . At the same time, James D. Wolfensohn, the president of the World Bank, in his Annual Meeting Speech to the IMF and the World Bank, stated that as many as half of the global population, i.e. about 3 billion people, live on less than USD 2 a day, and as many as 1.3 billion people on less that USD 1 a day (Wolfensohn 1999). In addition, we know that nearly 1 billion people in the world go hungry every day.

The situation in Africa is the most appalling. It is estimated that in the year 2,000 nearly one third of the global poor living on less that USD 1 a day will live in Africa, the majority in the rural areas. Africa is one of the few regions in which the relative share of poor people is still increasing, in spite of a process of comprehensive economic and political reform, initiated from the early 1980s onwards. According to the 1999 World Bank report, "Poverty Trends and Voices of the Poor", Eastern Europe is also experiencing a deepening of poverty. Here those living below one dollar a day rose from 1.1 million in 1987

---

[*] Throughout the introduction references of this type refer to the subsequent chapter by the person named.

to 23 million in 1998. In terms of absolute poor Latin America's record improved between 1990 and 1993 but deteriorated between 1996 (76 million) and 1998 (78 million). The figures for South Asia showed only marginal reductions between 1993 and 1996. Poverty has increased in South East Asia, especially Indonesia, following the Asian crisis.

These seminar proceedings comprise, in addition to the introduction, seven major contributions to the seminar, ordered in 8 chapters. When most seminar contributions had been received in written form, it was decided to produce a comprehensive seminar report in order to share the important issues, ideas and experiences with a broader concerned audience. Some contributions were updated and modified in order to capture more recent and critical developments related to the issue of poverty eradication, alleviation and reduction in rural Africa.

Major seminar issues

Increased Swedish emphasis on poverty reduction and alleviation

During the second half of the 1990s, the Swedish government formulated several new key policies on Africa. White Papers related to Africa presented to the Parliament included a new integrated Africa policy comprising the new partnership concept on poverty reduction and democratisation and human rights. In all these policies poverty issues are central and Sweden takes a broad view on poverty. The policies argue that the perceptions of the poor themselves have to constitute the important starting point for poverty eradication and poverty alleviation measures. Significant emphasis is placed on institutional aspects pertaining to African rural poverty, describing it as lack of access to and control over the political, economic and social resources required for providing people with security, capacity and opportunities (Karlsson).

Opportunities and barriers for poor smallholders emerging from the reforms

One important point of departure for the seminar was the wide experiences gained by IFAD as regards the dynamic development of the institutional context of poverty under economic and political reforms (Al-Sultan and Howe). The emphasis was on the one hand on the emergence of new opportunities from economic and political liberalisation, and on the other the barriers to smallholders benefiting from these opportunities.

IFAD's experience in rural Africa stems from its financing of projects to the tune of USD 2 billion, about 40 per cent of its total project financing by 1998. IFAD does not implement projects itself but works through other implementing agencies or organisations, such as government, NGOs and community associations. Total investment costs for the African projects amount to USD 4.5 billion.

They have all been focused on rural poor smallholder agriculture, research and extension, credit, social and economic infrastructure and community development (Al-Sultan).

A key lesson emerging from IFAD's experience is that the only sustainable way of poverty reduction is through helping the poor produce more and thus gain higher incomes. The reforms, according to IFAD, have created opportunities for such a scenario, but only given that certain conditions can be met. These are in particular linked to the need for poor rural smallholders to create organisations so that they can capture the benefits by improving their access to credit, better technologies and enhanced marketing opportunities. Smallholders also need improved conditions for negotiating or bargaining with local and international buyers, processors and investors and higher government administrative levels.

Emphasis is put on the need for rural producers to make use of comparative advantages and produce efficiently in order to be able to meet the increased international competition in agricultural products and raw materials. A key condition for smallholder success is their ability to link up with the private sector for upstream processing and access to credit and capital for required investments.

The institutional support provided by IFAD is said to be crucial and it is two-fold; it helps promote co-operation and organisation among the poor themselves and it helps to strengthen the local communities in their interaction with higher levels of administration and production, be they governmental or private.

The question could however be raised, whether IFAD romanticises the capacity of the rural poor to organise themselves, seize market opportunities and relate with private trading and credit institutions. The role of the state in improving conditions in rural areas is downplayed and the private sector is not taking any particular interest. The conclusion put forward is that the poor have to raise themselves through traditional and new structures and with external support (Howe).

The politics of reform and poverty alleviation

Whereas IFAD emphasised the need to help poor smallholders capture the potential benefits of reforms, others argued that this process was not realistically conceptualised. In addition there were problems inherent in the reforms themselves that hindered such benefits from emerging. The question was raised why two decades of reform activities and massive foreign assistance had failed to stem the tide of poverty in rural Africa (Havnevik and Mustapha).

Emphasising the linkages between reforms and institutions on the one hand, and institutions and poverty on the other, the argument is put forward that the reforms were flawed both in terms of their conceptualisation of the problems, the policy choices made and in the implementation of the policies (Mustapha).

A critical analysis is made of the World Bank strategy to alleviate poverty through pursuit of growth through labour intensive activities, provision of basic social services and the creation of safety nets for the most disadvantaged rural dwellers through targeted transfers. Repeatedly the assumption underlying the poverty alleviating strategies, that growth will be interlinked with increased public welfare, is questioned. In contrast to IFAD's approach, which puts emphasis on organisational capacity in order to enhance the technical, managerial and bargaining aspects of smallholders, mention is made of the high explanatory value of political organisation for poverty alleviation.

The political argument is also raised as a critique against the vision of the politics of economic reform that there is a clear correspondence between economic interest and political orientation. Closer scrutiny of the economic, political and social terrain of African rural areas, shows that ideological, cultural and historical factors are as important as structural ones in influencing political alliances. The reforms basically see people's motivation to be linked to immediate material interest, so that policies to benefit the poor are only acceptable to the non-poor if the non-poor benefit too. In the end the implication is that the poor are left with little initiative of their own, basically their only freedom is their ability to support reform programmes (Mustapha).

*Constraints and opportunities on access to economic, social and political
resources*

The seminar discussed as well constraints and opportunities related to access to economic, social and political resources from the point of view of the legal system, with particular focus on women (Rwebangira) and regarding the character and role of indigenous rural institutions, i.e. systems, values and regulations that people apply to shape repeated human interaction (Havnevik). The latter institutions would be systems of customary land tenure and associated inheritance rights that have emerged from within African rural history in conjunction with the impact of colonial rule.

Both the legal system and indigenous rural institutions tend to be highly discriminatory against women, allowing the major producers of foodstuffs in most African countries only partial control of the products that emanate from their labour. It is argued that women, due to the customary and legal constraints to ownership, are unable to lift their aspirations above the objective of subsistence, thus holding back a major force from the development of rural production and development (Rwebangira).

Very different perspectives are reported as to the character and role of indigenous institutions in rural Africa. Where major external agencies see the need to create new institutions either to promote a market based strategy or to enhance and protect smallholders in order that they will reap the potential benefits of the reforms, others argue that indigenous institutions already exist with important influence over rural people's scope for choice both as regards production, exchange, negotiations and relationships (Berry, 1993 and Mamdani, 1996). Overlooking the complexity and impact of such institutions may make assistance efforts, albeit well meaning for the poor, ineffective. This is because rural people's livelihood may be more conditioned by reducing insecurity through maintaining and developing social relationships, i.e. implying a bias towards investing in relationships rather than in productive activities. This could obstruct the drive for accumulation and expanded production in the rural sector, and instead imply lateral circulation of value(s), for instance in the form of converting between spheres of economic, political and social capital (Hårsmar, 1998 and Seppälä, 1998).

Development assistance and poverty eradication and alleviation

The increasing focus on poverty alleviation and eradication in Africa reflects the growing importance accorded to these issues by nearly all actors, both internal and external to Africa.

Development assistance has for its part attempted to find new modes of relating to recipient countries, institutions and people. The urge by external donors to develop civil society as a force in development and poverty alleviation was initiated in the late 1980s and gained further impetus through the wave of multiparty democratisation in the 1990s. The latter process also led to increasing focus on, and efforts to bring about, a more decentralised government bureaucracy and shifting donor funds to lower levels, i.e. as close as possible to the beneficiaries. Both IFAD and others have shown scepticism as to the impact of democratisation in the rural areas, arguing that most of the positive impact might have been captured by the urban elite (Howe). Budget driven adjustment programmes have on the other hand led to withdrawal of state provided services, while the local sector remains weak and hesitant about rural investment.

As many inherent problems related to development assistance had not been resolved, donors for their part, stimulated by the response of the receivers of assistance, started to seriously discuss ownership of reforms and implement partnership ideas in development assistance relations and activities (Karlsson). Putting such a partnership into practice for poverty eradication is, however, not simple (Booth). Who defines the parameters of the partnership, what are the criteria for qualifying as a partner, how can some kind of equality be attained in the partnership when most of the material resources are in the hands of one side? Viewing partnership from the angle of poverty eradication, what are the dilemmas, trade-offs and sequences involved (Booth)? Putting partnership on the development assistance agenda, as has been done by the Swedish government, Nordic donors and other concerned countries as well as by major international institutions, including IFAD, must necessarily be a step in the right direction. It reflects a growing respect for the relationship between north and south, although much remains to be resolved in order to arrive at workable solutions.

However, recent events indicate that further positive signs are emerging within development assistance and reform thinking that may allow the partnership concept to gain strength. Not least does this appear in the recent IMF/World Bank Annual Meeting Speech by the president of the World Bank (Wolfensohn, 1999) where he underlines the crucial importance of "good governance" for poverty alleviation world-wide. Further he underlines the need to establish a balance between macroeconomic and financial issues on the one hand and social and structural issues on the other. This coupled with firm support for debt relief and advocacy of a fair, comprehensive and inclusive trading system, may allow renewed attention to be given to the external and global dimension of low growth and poverty in Sub-Saharan Africa in particular and in the south in general (Mustapha).

A dialogue focusing on these broad and global issues will, if honestly conducted, allow the opening up for the critical investigation of the role of the north not only for biodiversity and global warming and the climate (which is very important), but also for the way our policies and the execution of our power and our lifestyles impact on the conditions for development of people in the South, but as well for the potential of our planet to become sustainable in the longer run.

Conclusions

One major poverty eradication approach emerging in the seminar was the one based on the practical experience and analytical capacity of IFAD. It puts strong emphasis on the potential space for poverty alleviation that has emerged through the productive opportunities created by the reforms for poor rural smallholders. This has led IFAD to formulate clear priorities and strategies for combating African rural poverty of which institutional support for smallholders is a critical element.

Another position emerging in the seminar argued that the reforms were flawed in themselves and as such did not provide the set of opportunities for smallholders identified by IFAD. Emphasis was rather on the political significance of smallholder organisation for poverty eradication. A third view related poverty eradication to the need to undo legal and various forms of access constraints on the poor, for example, legal constraints are still effectively discriminating the major producers, women, in terms of access to various assets and this is often exacerbated by the working of indigenous institutions. The three positions mentioned were not entirely exclusive, the above underlines their major focus.

The first two perspectives both emphasised the changing conditions that had emerged for African smallholders as a result of economic and political reforms during the last two decades, however, they assessed the process and the outcome differently. The third view focused more on internal and domestic constraints to smallholder development and poverty eradication. The different perspectives that emerged in the seminar as regards poverty alleviation also seem to be related to different conceptions and emphases about the institutional context in rural Africa. This was reflected in the different focuses that the various positions afforded to formal institutions and their roles on the one hand and indigenous institutions on the other. One important outcome of the seminar thus seems to be the need to investigate more deeply the contrasts between the different positions on the institutional context of rural Africa and reflect on what the outcome of this might imply for future policies and strategies for poverty eradication in rural areas.

References

Berry, Sara (1993): *No Condition Is Permanent. The Social Dynamics of Agrarian Change in Sub-Saharan Africa.* Madison, the University of Wisconsin Press.

Hårsmar, Mats (1998): "Institutions and Investment—a Search for Output Response in Sub-Saharan African Agriculture". (mimeo).

Mamdani, Mahmood (1996): *Citizen and Subject. Contemporary Africa and the Legacy of Late Colonialism.* Princeton Studies in Culture/Power/History. Princeton University Press, Princeton, New Jersey.

Seppälä, Pekka (1998): *Diversification and Accumulation in Rural Tanzania.* Nordic Africa Institute, Uppsala, Sweden.

Wolfensohn, James D. (1999): "Coalition for Change". Annual Meeting Speech, IMF/World Bank Annual Meeting, September 28, Washington D.C.

Chapter 2
Issues, Experiences and Options for Eradicating Poverty in Rural Africa: Opening Statement

Mats Karlsson

It is with great pleasure that I wish you all, on behalf of the Swedish Government, the Department of Rural Development Studies (at the Swedish University of Agricultural Sciences) and the Nordic Africa Institute, a warm and heartfelt welcome. It is most gratifying to find so many personalities here today who are so significantly involved in the fight against rural poverty.

As you all know, IFAD celebrates twenty years of operations in 1998. And we have chosen to use this anniversary to illuminate the complex issues to which IFAD has devoted its full attention and to which all of us are committed: issues concerning poverty reduction in rural Africa that ought to be considered basic although they are often gravely overlooked, issues concerning the consequences for the poor of reform, institutions and access to assets.

In this context I would like to pay a special tribute to IFAD's President, Fawzi Al-Sultan. His dedication and vision have greatly strengthened IFAD's ability to be an important actor in the fight against poverty. Sweden is proud to have been able to play an active role in facilitating the recent restructuring of IFAD and the replenishment of IFAD's resources. This seminar is but one expression of our strong belief in IFAD's mission.

Before we commence our discourse on various theories, opinions and strategies, I think it is important to remember what is at stake, the rights and livelihoods of poor women, men and children in Africa. In spite of the "African renaissance", the picture of rural poverty in Africa remains bleak. I will not relate the horrific facts and figures we all know all too well. Suffice it to say, the chasm between rich and poor continues to widen; we can still not rest assured that poor people's livelihoods can be sustained; and the rights of the poor are all too often breached and violated.

IFAD knows all this and has better than any other agency stayed true to its mandate and objectives of reducing rural poverty while the winds of change, political climates, demands of public opinion and the whims of fashion have caused development agencies to drift, sometimes steering away from the immediate concern for rural people's livelihoods.

IFAD is a unique organisation. Its distinctive feature is the combination of innovation and resource mobilisation. The strength of IFAD lies in its ability to organise and manage smooth interaction between these components and to respond to practical challenges and the demands of reality.

IFAD's work can be seen as a catalyst, a creator of possibilities by means of inventing and contributing extra resources which are crucial to help those innovative approaches to survive and to start to grow. We look forward to hearing how it can be a pathfinder toward sustained rural poverty reduction. We need to share experiences about which paths to walk: innovative thinking provided the concepts; institutions were given attention; participation was seen as essential; understanding the gender dimension and female poverty was regarded as crucial; and poor people's access to assets was considered imperative.

It is this conviction, too, which constitutes the foundation both for Sweden's work in the field of poverty reduction and for this seminar.

Like others, the Swedish government has reflected on the complexities inherent in poverty reduction and the interlinkages with democratisation and respect for human rights. We have reflected on the overall changes in Africa. A two-year long effort resulted in April 1998 in a White Paper to Parliament on a new integrated Africa Policy. Two other White Papers, on poverty reduction and democratisation and human rights, were completed during 1997.

In these policy documents, Sweden takes a broad view of poverty. The perceptions of the poor themselves have to constitute the starting point. Poverty is described as a lack of access to and control over political, economic and social resources which are necessary to provide people with security, capacity and opportunities.

Security against unforeseen events such as sickness, accidents, natural disasters, unemployment, injustice, violence within and outside the family, and economic and political crises, as well as security in old age is a fundamental human need. Security can be achieved, for instance, through traditional social networks, social security systems and benefits and social, political and economic rights guaranteed under international conventions and laws.

People can improve their *capacity* by developing their own resources in the form of income, savings, health, knowledge and skills or other assets.

Their *opportunities* for taking control of their lives are often determined by social conditions concerning, for example, civil liberties and human rights, participation in decision-making processes and economic policies.

The common denominator is access to assets. Both material assets goods and services that build human capital; markets; labour; land; finance and credit and intangible assets, that is, social and political capital. As David Booth has expressed it: "Treating the assets of the poor as capital, as stocks that can be created, stored, exchanged and depleted provides a powerful entry point into the causal explanations of poverty."

The interlinkages between the political, economic and institutional spheres will be discussed. The linkages between the social, cultural, and ethnic spheres and the wider society will also be emphasised since this diversity tends to guide and influence important elements of rural development.

This will throw some light on the role of local and indigenous institutions as bearers of power, norms and values in obstructing or channelling agricultural development, and on social relations as important channels for negotiating access to resources.

A fundamental concern during a decade of adjustment has been why the effects have not been as positive as anticipated. Some of the answers are well known, such as the lack of ownership. Others have been less well penetrated, such as the effects of macro policies on the micro level, the whole question of supply-response, gender issues, time allocation and micro institutional issues. Some of these complex realities are well documented others are not. But the linkage between understanding and translating into overall analysis and, more importantly, into policy conclusions is far from evident.

Subsequently the seminar will attempt to translate policy into practice. We will aim at realising the concept of partnership, and focus on how to make partnerships inclusive rather than exclusive, and forceful as bonds against poverty.

By the concept of partnership we mean the endeavour in co-operation with our African partners to establish a more equal relationship, one that builds upon mutual respect and a more explicit code of conduct. In that partnership both African and Swedish resources will be utilised with the aim of making the African partners the subjects of their own destiny and not the object of someone else's design. A true partnership must also be based on certain openly accounted for and jointly discussed values. The point of departure for a dialogue on partnership is that attention and consideration must be given to historical, social and cultural conditions. In the dialogue a minimum set of common values must make up the platform. These shared values are based on universal human rights and poverty reduction as a *sine qua non*. A true partnership cannot be restricted to a small number of African leaders but has to be inclusive including the private sector, civil society, and legitimate representatives of poor women and men.

As to strategies and instruments in the fight against poverty we have four guiding principles in our methodological work:

– to strive to integrate economic, political, social, cultural and gender perspectives, analytically, methodologically and in practical development co-operation activities;

– to strive to incorporate both micro and macro perspectives in analyses and policy;

– to work in a cross sectional manner;

– to promote the use of participatory approaches in all development work in order to incorporate the perspectives of both female and male stakeholders and in particular the knowledge, values and priorities of people living in poverty.

Simplistic as these principles might sound, their implementation is the key to success.

It is these issues, in theory and in practice, which this seminar will revolve around. They will also, I hope, shed light upon how we can share ideas, agree on methodology and achieve the necessary co-ordination and cohesion in our common approach to poverty eradication.

I also believe that this meeting between policy makers, practitioners and researchers from many different agencies and institutions will be creative and invigorating, be a source of new ideas and act as a stimulus for future action.

Chapter 3
IFAD's Experiences from Two Decades of Poverty Alleviation in Rural Africa

Fawzi H. Al-Sultan

The topic chosen for the Seminar is particularly apt as Africa has throughout these last twenty years been a major focus of our operations, with some 40 per cent of IFAD resources earmarked for this region. Africa is one of the few regions in the world where the proportion of poor is still rising, the bulk of them living in rural areas, subject to chronic hunger, vulnerability and deprivation.

Over the last twenty years IFAD has supported some 496 projects in 112 developing countries providing nearly USD 5 billion towards their total investment costs of USD 17 billion. On full development these projects are expected to help some thirty million households, two hundred million poor people, to achieve sustainable livelihoods and food security. Drawing on this experience we have found that there are several key dimensions to addressing poverty, starting from the perspective that the key to viable poverty alleviation lies with the poor themselves and their own under-utilised talents and capacities.

The first element is strengthening the capacity of the poor to organise themselves and gain a voice in local decision making and resource allocation that will enable them to express their priorities and help formulate the responses.

Second, we must promote both a favourable macro environment as well as a supportive micro environment for the poor and help forge more efficient linkages between the two.

Third, a central part of these linkages is the challenge of involving private sector entities as investors and service providers.

Fourth, in order to ensure gender balance and participatory development, advantage should be taken of the new opportunities arising from the transformation of economic and political systems.

IFAD is unusual among multilateral agencies in having an exclusive focus on rural poverty. The key lesson we have understood in our twenty years of operations is that the only sustainable way to reduce poverty is to help the poor produce more and gain higher incomes. Given that in rural Africa, production is overwhelmingly in smallscale farm units, poverty eradication has to be based on smallholder farmers, particularly women farmers.

This has also meant going to zones where the poor live, often the most marginal areas prone to degradation. Moreover, in a region where women produce the bulk of food and contribute significantly to household incomes, ensuring that women have fair access to project services is not only an ethical concern but an economic imperative.

Over the last twenty years, under its Regular Programme and the Special Programme for Sub-Saharan African Countries, IFAD has helped finance projects in Sub-Saharan Africa providing some USD 2 billion for the total investment costs of these projects of about USD 4.5 billion. All of this investment was focused on the rural poor and smallholder agriculture, in programmes for research and extension, credit, social and economic infrastructure, and community development. In our operations we have given particular attention to involving the poor, not only in designing the projects but also in implementing them. Such participation makes the projects more responsive to the real needs of the poor as well as allows them to gain the experience of managing development initiatives. The latter is sometimes as important for their future as the actual gains in income and production that the project brings about.

A decade ago the formal monetary economy in much of Sub-Saharan Africa was not so much a market economy as an administered system imposing unfair terms of trade on the rural sector. This is a major reason underlying the failure of so many rural development programmes in the past. Fortunately, this situation has changed dramatically in recent years. Markets have been liberalised, and exchange rates are at more reasonable levels. For the first time in three decades the small farmer has the possibility to sell at a fair price, to save and to invest. What this means is that the rural poor and their communities have the prospect of increasing the resources that they directly control to invest in their own development.

This is the "up" side of macro reforms. Yet there is a "down" side. Budget driven adjustment programmes have led to the withdrawal of state-provided services in many rural areas, while the local private sector remains weak and hesitant about rural investment. Paradoxically even as the African poor in agriculture are offered new possibilities of income and development, the means to reach them have eroded. Overcoming this gap is one of our major tasks. It will require promoting the flow of resources and provision of services to the rural poor, and helping develop new linkages and partnerships that will allow the poor to become the principal agents of change.

In these efforts we need to ask, "Who are our development partners today?" Governments of course continue to play an important role. But increasingly the policy of most governments in Africa is not to be the main force of rural development, but to be the facilitator. The question is who or what is to be the engine of transformation?

The first answer is the small farmer and the small farmer community. Here we are talking about community management of natural resources, especially in extensive agricultural systems. We are talking about community mechanisms for savings mobilisation and credit. And we are talking about community control over local level public spending. But we have to be careful since local communities comprise different groups with varying interests.

General development support is often pre-empted by non-poor groups and the trickle down to the poor is neither assured nor rapid. It is for this reason that careful but intelligent targeting of assistance has been one of the defining characteristics of IFAD's approach. We aim our programmes directly at poor communities, especially the more disadvantaged groups. A key group in this context is women, who are often the backbone of the rural economy. Throughout our operations our prime objective is ensuring that poor groups can develop the organisation necessary to articulate their views and assure their position in the development process.

In effect, we want poor people to be able to sustain and control local organisations and resources shaped by their needs and interests in the context of the conditions in which they live. This should provide the real content and micro level counterpart to the large-scale process of political democratisation. Without such local level changes democratisation is likely to remain incomplete for the poor. Our partnership with the NGOs has been crucial in this area, not only in terms of collaborating in projects, but in developing what one might call the social fabric of the poor. However, this sort of local institutional development cannot take place in isolation from the larger relationships in which local communities find themselves.

Our institutional support therefore has a twofold aim. The first is to help promote collaborative relations and organisation among the poor themselves. Here, harmonising the interests of the poor and less poor groups in the community sometimes poses a serious challenge. The benefits of helping the poor to organise themselves to act will be eroded if this causes other groups to work against it. We have found that in Africa working through local traditional structures can often limit such difficulties but we need to keep striving to make it understood that at local levels, as at others, improving the conditions of the poor does not pose a threat to the well-being of the less poor. Poverty eradication does not need to be a zero value game, either within nations or among them.

Our second aim is to strengthen the capacity of the local communities and their organisations to interact positively with upstream regional and national institutions. As we have noted earlier such linkages are essential for the poor to be able to enter into the mainstream of the market economy in a meaningful and fair way.

Participatory community organisation helps to create a basis for poverty eradication. But it is not enough on its own. Consider the implications of market liberalisation. Farmers increasingly have to pay international prices for their inputs including capital. They also receive prices for their output that are influenced by international prices. Smallholder production can be remunerative under these conditions only if it is competitive. Otherwise smallholder farmers will be further marginalized and their poverty worsened. Yet even optimal use of local resources and existing technologies cannot always ensure a competitive position, especially when markets in many rural areas are underdeveloped and sometimes unfair.

Usually higher levels of competitiveness will require expanded access to improved technology, as well as capital, together with support from more efficient trading and processing services. Governments are now less able to promote such conditions. Nor is it likely that NGOs can pass from their important role in supporting local organisation and mobilisation to fill this gap. In many cases sustained smallholder development will require association with private sector suppliers for credit and services.

In the past, this aspect was neglected. In today's market driven development process however, we must think in terms of growing private sector investments. But it would be a mistake to look at this issue as one of community development versus the smallholder private sector partnership. Our strategy preparation for Mozambique, for example, has indicated that community organisations and associations are essential to establish a fair deal for smallholders. This echoes historical experience in Northern Europe and the United States where agricultural co-operatives played an important role in ensuring that the benefits of agricultural development were shared. Moreover in some conditions, particularly in marginal ecologically vulnerable areas, community resource management and mobilisation are the sole means of sustainable improvements in rural poverty.

Nonetheless, we have to recognise that private investment on a significant scale, both national and international, is one of the main contemporary forces in developing systems of production. A failure to associate smallscale producers in Africa with these movements will limit their capacity to achieve competitive production and leave them on the margins of the economy.

In East and Southern Africa we are beginning to address this challenge. In Uganda for example an IFAD project has brought together a commercial oil mill operation with smallholder cultivators of palm trees with the former providing technical support to the farmers to improve yields. On a pan-regional basis we are using IFAD grant financing to develop financial linkages between commercial financial institutions and local micro credit institutions. This builds on our experience in Asian countries like Indonesia and India where informal savings and credit institutions have been successfully linked to commercial banks. A third instance comes from Zimbabwe where we are providing grants to NGOs to strengthen smallscale trading networks in rural areas. We are also launching a larger programme to support the expansion of rural trading networks in a number of central and East African countries including Zambia and Mozambique.

These examples highlight the potential for involving the private sector in poverty alleviation efforts. Nonetheless, we have a long way to go in tapping this potential. There is I believe a considerable scope for collaboration between multilateral and bilateral donors in this field of growing importance.

Recognising the role of market processes does not of course mean that we have to weaken our fundamental aim of empowering the poor, especially women, in the process of social and economic development. What it does mean is that we have to understand how issues like gender evolve as the economic structure undergoes transformation. Do we, for example, help women and household food security more effectively by focusing on domestic subsistence production or by promoting increased engagement by women in off farm production and services? There are no universal answers here, what is important is to be sensitive and responsive to the specific conditions and needs of those we intend to assist.

Poverty issues today receive a much higher priority and attention than was the case a decade ago. This is a welcome development for an institution like IFAD which for many years was virtually the sole international financial institution to give central attention to poverty.

But the sad fact is that even as the rhetoric has sharpened on poverty, actual support for agricultural and rural development has fallen. Yet the bulk of the poor, some three quarters by a recent World Bank estimate, live in rural areas drawing their uncertain livelihoods from agriculture and related activities. All of us committed to poverty eradication need to face this paradox by working to reverse the declining support for rural development on the one hand and combining our resources and action to multiply our overall impact on the other.

Within the UN system there are major efforts under way to tap the synergy between different UN organisations. But we need to do more to strengthen collaboration between bilateral and multilateral donors. Given the strong focus of the Nordic countries on poverty alleviation, IFAD and your countries have a great scope to reinforce co-operation in Africa. Nordic countries provide a significant part of development assistance to Sub-Saharan Africa, and in many of them, IFAD is the major international institution providing financing for rural development. In this connection, I am glad to note that we have started to liaise more closely with regard to natural resource management, decentralisation, small scale irrigation and rural finance development. I look forward to more joint and parallel programmes in these areas. I am sure that the discussions in this Seminar will help to create greater awareness of each other's capacities to bring this about.

Operational collaboration between us should be complemented with joint efforts at the policy level as well. Clearly poverty alleviation cannot be achieved without political stability. Unfortunately in many areas of Sub-Saharan Africa civil strife, instability and weak governance are a common feature. In the last few years African countries have started to make brave efforts to redress this situation. Their efforts deserve support both directly and by helping to promote sustainable poverty alleviation. Policy dialogue should not be limited to just the guardians of the world financial order. Those of us concerned with poverty, that is with empowering the poor, particularly women, also need to play a role. In this regard, we would be happy to see a closer consultation with the Nordic countries to identify the key policy areas relevant to our concerns, and speak jointly on such issues.

One specific example is the question of debt which needs to be addressed in ways that actively support poverty alleviation. This has been the spirit in which IFAD has decided to participate in the Heavily Indebted Poor Countries Debt Initiative (HIPC). We have tried to ensure that the conditions imposed in HIPC give stimulus to production by the poor rather than merely lead to further cut-backs in the support and services available to them. The Nordic countries have a similar perspective as ours on this issue and I look forward to continuing our co-operation in this area.

Working with the countries of Africa, I believe that a coherent and imaginative effort on the part of donors could make a difference. This is why this Seminar is particularly important. Not just as a celebration of IFAD's twenty years, but as an expression of our joint interest to devise new solutions, and to apply them. Over the next two days we should establish what we know and what we need to know, what is being done, and what should be done.

Another area that deserves our attention is working to raise the level of development resources, particularly assistance for rural development and poverty alleviation. Sweden and the other Nordic countries have been major financial supporters of IFAD and they have been strong allies in our shared goal of ending poverty and hunger. We look forward to your continued support to IFAD, especially in the context of the replenishment of the Fund's resources.

The 1990s have been a difficult period for Africa. Today however there are a growing number of indications that offer cause for hope. New governments in many countries promise more democratic societies and new policy approaches have opened opportunities to reverse the dismal trends of past years. I am sure that the insights generated by this Seminar will help all of us to grasp this opportunity more effectively.

Chapter 4
The Politics of Economic Reforms: Implications for Institutions and Poverty in the Rural African Setting

Abdul Raufu Mustapha

Introduction

After two decades of economic reforms under structural adjustment, poverty continues to stalk the peoples and countries of Africa. In a late 1999 address to the Organization of African Trade Union Unity in Johannesburg, Nelson Mandela described poverty in Africa as the 'number one problem facing the world'. For his part, James Wolfensohn, President of the World Bank, urged the 1999 Annual General Meeting of the Bank and the International Monetary Fund to consider poverty alleviation and debt relief as the two major planks on which the world economic order should be built in the 21st Century. Such high level concern indicates the severity of the problem. As we contemplate future efforts at tackling the problem, it is perhaps pertinent to ask why two decades of economic reforms have so far failed to stem the tide of poverty in Africa? In this contribution, I intend to examine the economic reforms starting in the 1980s and the political reforms starting in the 1990s. Emphasis will be on two inter-linked themes: reforms and institutions, and institutions and poverty. My central argument, consistent with most of the literature on the issue, is that the reform effort was critically flawed. Flaws abound in the conceptualisation of the problems to be tackled, the policy choices made, and implementation of these policies. Above all, there was a failure to understand or come to terms with the formal and informal institutional matrix within which the reforms were being carried out. And it is this connection between reforms, institutions, and poverty, particularly in rural Africa, that I try to explore.

Poverty and the institutional framework of economic reforms

In the 1950s and 1960s, African countries were encouraged to follow a policy of economic growth as a means of tackling the problem of poverty and deprivation. The idea was that the benefits of growth would ultimately trickle down to the poor. The role of the state was central in these national projects of societal transformation. By the 1970s, however, the failure of this policy in sustaining economic growth and tackling poverty was becoming apparent. Policy emphasis shifted to redistribution with growth (RWG). The adoption of RWG led to increased provision of social services to the poor. In the 1960s and the 1970s, many African countries registered improvements in their social indicators. By the 1980s, however, the crises in many African economies led to a new approach to tackling poverty within the overall rubric of structural adjustment. Since the 1980s, most African countries have undergone reforms in their economies inspired by this liberalising philosophy of the World Bank and the IMF. Between 1980 and 1989, an estimated 241 SAPs were initiated by various African governments. The persistence of poverty by 1990 led to renewed efforts by the Bank to confront the problem. This renewed interest was signalled by the publication of the *World Development Report* (WDR) on Poverty in 1990 (World Bank, 1990), followed thereafter by the publication of *Poverty Assessment Reports* (PARs) on more than twenty African countries after 1990.

The strategy of the Bank, consistent with its liberalising philosophy, consists of three basic parts. Firstly, the pursuit of growth through labour intensive activities which are expected to favour the poor since labour is the one asset the poor have in abundance. Secondly, the provision of basic social services like primary education and basic health coverage to the poor. Thirdly, a safety net for the weakest members of society through targeted transfers. This was both a strategy for renewed growth and poverty alleviation. A primary institutional plank for this strategy was the establishment of a market friendly macroeconomic framework. This advocacy of the market is directly related to a negative perception of the role of the state in managing the economy and tackling poverty. Government policies are seen to be leading to market distortions which prevent access to income-earning opportunities for the poor. Labour-market regulations reduce labour demand while public expenditure programmes are not well targeted and not cost effective.

The strategy is to promote the best opportunities for earning an income through the deregulation of markets while the marketization of health and education through private provision and user charges will improve the efficiency and reach of service provision. The view was that supply-led service provision often produced goods which the consumer did not want, and this was often done in an inefficient manner. Service provision was to be demand-led, the demand coming from the increased earning opportunities for the poor generated by the changes in the macroeconomic environment. Harnessing market opportunities and incentives is seen as the best way to tackle poverty. For the old, disabled and those living in resource poor regions, a safety net should be provided. Targeting is a key factor.

The central institution for this strategy is the market, particularly the market for labour. Poverty alleviation is seen in terms of increased opportunities for remunerative employment. The productive use of labour is seen in utilitarian terms—labour is seen not as a human activity but as an alienable asset. Macro-economic reform will make it possible for the poor to convert their labour into effective demand for goods and services. This macroeconomic package has so far produced disappointing results. A major problem is the real returns to low-skilled labour in many African economies. Hanmer et al. (1997) poignantly point out in their assessment of the Bank's *Poverty Assessment Reports*, that there was never an attempt to understand the real and concrete relationship between the returns to unskilled labour and the subsistence costs confronting the poor in any country in which the policy was being implemented. A second problem is the assumed connection between market-driven growth and public welfare. In this regard, Hanmer et al. also point out that the PARs fail to question the valid-ity of the assertion that economic growth will necessarily lead to poverty reduction or that private investment will necessarily lead to the service of public objectives. For their part, Dreze and Sen (1989, 258), point out that there were massive public welfare improvements in China at a time of moderate growth before the initiation of liberalising reforms in 1979. After 1979, growth accelerated, but this was paradoxically accompanied by a crisis of public provi-sioning and increased mortality. Growth and improved public welfare are not necessarily related. In Africa, the impact of market-driven growth on the ability of the poor to secure their welfare remains problematic. One Bank document candidly observes that:

> The Bank's central operating paradigm,…, is the 'miracle of the market'—those who need goods and services offer prices that stimulate others to supply them. This prin-ciple of demand organises service delivery to the rich and powerful, whose pur-chasing power or connections stimulate those services that interest them (Salmen, 1992, 1).

Of course, it cannot be argued that the market has no role to play either in the reform of African economies or in the alleviation of poverty. Dreze and Sen (1989, 76, fn 24) point out the role of 'extensive pre-capitalist regional systems of exchange' in pre-colonial East Africa and the Sahel in safeguarding societies against threats to subsistence. And no observer of the predatory excesses of the post-colonial African state can deny the vital importance of market signals in the proper management of macroeconomic life. The problem is the particular way the market has been privileged in the reform process as a miraculous panacea for Africa's economic woes. In the current African context, it would seem that unquestioning belief in the miracle of the market has been just as harmful to the poor as excessive state intervention.

The second institutional plank of the reform process is the provision of a safety net. Those who cannot avail themselves of the new opportunities offered by the market are supposedly to be taken care of by the provision of this safety net. Though there is the passing acknowledgement of the responsibility of gov-ernments in aiding distressed communities in times of insecurity (*WDR*, 1990, 90), the core institutions underwriting this safety net are expected to be local communities (individuals, families, community based organisations and whole communities) and local and international NGOs. The *WDR*, 1990, suggests that the needs of the poor are best served by flexible programmes involving the intended beneficiaries. Such programmes build institutions, employ NGOs and community based groups, and respond to local needs. Questions have, however, been raised about the limitations of this institutional format, particularly with respect to the ability of individuals, communities and NGOs to provide an adequate safety net. According to the Bank:

> Individuals, families, and communities have ways of coping with poverty. Individuals and families redistribute and stabilise consumption, diversify income sources, migrate, and give and receive transfers. In many parts of Sub-Saharan Africa the term for being poor is synonymous with lacking kin or friends. At the community level these 'social security' arrangements are sometimes quite sophisticated (*WDR*, 1990, 90).

However, the *WDR*, 1990, goes on to acknowledge the gradual dissolution of • communal solidarity and support systems as group ties weaken. These points are again made in the various PARs. If group solidarity is to be relied upon for a safety net and this solidarity is observed to be decomposing, then policy ought to address the possibility of their long-term maintenance or reconstitution. Significantly, nothing is said about what is to be done in the face of this gradual institutional dissolution (Hanmer et al. 1997, xi). The critical problem here is the bland conceptualisation of these local communities. What we have is an *ab initio* conceptualisation of local communities as depoliticised entities and local participation is seen in purely managerial terms with the main objective of servicing project needs. The internal structures and tensions of these local communities are hardly explored. Their implications for the safety net are not addressed. What, for example, are the positive and negative implications of the complex web of patron-client networks which permeate many local communities? What is the gender and welfare implication of male migration? In reality, local communities are often left to their own devices or to NGOs which play an increasing role in the Bank's operations.

Between 1972 and 87, NGOs were involved in about 15 Bank projects. In 1989 alone, they were involved in 50 such projects (Salmen, 1992, 16). The basic thinking behind this increased involvement, apart from the distrust of public action by the state, is the principle of intermediation between development agencies and their client, beneficiary populations:

> Bureaucracies and technology, on one side, and grassroots institutions and culture, on the other, too often fail to come together at a central common ground. The catalyst can play a most effective brokerage role in bringing these more and less formal kinds of institutions and their derivatives to first understanding and then concerted action (Salmen, 1992, 17).

It is postulated that this intermediation between the informal institutions and cultural universe of the poor, on the one hand, and the complex technological world of formal institutions, on the other, will provide both income generating opportunities and emergency relief to the poor. The NGOs are also considered to be the best means of efficient service delivery to needy communities. However, studies by Bank staff suggest that this intermediation, particularly with governmental bureaucracies, is not working:

> The emerging wisdom on NGOs is that they are most effective when working in close association with the communities of the poor and the bureaucracies of government. Few NGOs, however, appear to perform this dual micro-macro task well, for lack of commitment, ability, or both. Judith Tendler's study on poverty alleviation in activities in livelihood, employment, and income generation found that NGO programs 'typically do not make significant inroads on poverty in a particular country'...(Salmen, 1992, 16).

This view is corroborated by a senior member of a northern NGO (Goyder 1997). He argues that increased aid flows through NGOs have not had the effect of reducing poverty. He suggests that large parts of Africa are simply not covered by local or international NGOs. By implication, both poverty reduction and emergency relief would be impossible in such neglected tracts. He also argues that 'NGOs, for all their valuable work, are now simply slowing down the rate at which life for the poor gets worse'. Lastly, he draws attention to an emerging 'credibility gap' between the optimistic rhetoric of northern NGOs as they seek to elicit contributions from their publics, and the pessimistic reality in the field in Africa.

It seems obvious that the institutional basis of the safety net in the economic reform process is rather shaky. Individual males may migrate, leaving their families in misery; patrons may cheat as well as help their clients; NGOs engage in admirable policy advocacy and service delivery, but without denting the general incidence of poverty. These possible scenarios suggest a problematization of local communities and their realistic role in the provision of a safety net. Another problem is that this safety net is implicitly seen as charity and the thrust is to mitigate the impact of poverty and not the integration of the poor into mainstream society. Even if it worked according to plan, this safety net would sustain life, but do little about the exclusion of the poor from critical aspects of social life. As the Bank noted:

> The poor are often set apart by cultural and educational barriers. Illiterate people may be intimidated by officials or may simply lack information about programs.... The poor play little part in politics and are often, in effect, disenfranchised (*WDR*, 1990, 37).

Poverty and the institutional framework of political reforms

In 1980, there were only five African countries with political systems that could be vaguely described as pluralist. From 1990, pluralist politics of differing hues and credibility, have emerged in the majority of African countries as a result of political reforms. In many instances, the reforms meant meaningful change; in some others, wily politicians learnt to speak the language of democracy while continuing with business as usual. What have been the institutional implications of these political reforms? What are their consequences for the incidence of poverty? The relevance of these questions lies in the suggestion by Reynolds, cited in Dethier (1999, 3), that 'the single most important explanatory variable (of development) is political organisation and the administrative competence of government'.

Though the economic and political reforms are distinct processes with different origins and motivations, they share many common features and premises. Furthermore, both packages have now converged, constituting elements in a unified perspective on reforming African countries. Initial concern with the African state examined issues of state capacity, bureaucratic organisation and the relationship of vested interest to the political process. The state was seen as bloated, over-extended, inefficient, and a tool of urban vested interests. The state's regulatory capacities were seen as weak, and the regulations themselves as dysfunctional. This problematic state was to be rolled back through a process of privatisation, decentralisation, dismantling of regulatory boards and civil service reforms. The spaces abandoned by the state were to be taken up by private economic interests and voluntary organisations like NGOs. The new 'governance' agenda which developed out of the convergence of the economic and political reform programmes seeks to explain how informational, transactional and political constraints on governmental action lead to trade-offs between efficiency and the extraction of rent by political actors, leading to welfare-increasing or welfare-decreasing outcomes (Dethier, 1999, 1). Technology, endowments and institutions (legal and political) are seen as the determinants of economic opportunities in society. States are always ready to prey on society and dictatorships in particular are sources of inefficiencies (Dethier, 1999, 6–12). The tone of the debate is both economistic and anti-state. Technocratic issues often take precedence over representational and solidaristic aspects of the state as an institution.

The specifically political element of this governance agenda sought to promote a 'tropicalized' version of democracy narrowly defined as multipartyism, a free press, and regular elections. Form was privileged over content. The divide between this political element and the strictly economic aspect was mediated by 'political conditionalities'. However, the politics of economic reform also had other distinctive features. Firstly, the economic crisis is largely seen as a consequence of policy failure, mismanagement and corruption internal to the African state. The external context is often downplayed. It is argued that the poor are often ignored by the state and any effort to get the state to adopt pro-poor policies would involve a trade-off, not between growth and poverty reduction, but between the poor and the 'non-poor'. However, it is also suggested that reforms that aim at poverty reduction need not pit the poor against this 'non-poor'. Though many economic policies benefit the rich at the expense of the poor, others link the fortunes of both groups. Policy coalitions, based on sectoral or regional interests are seen as the best way forward for the poor.

In my view, this vision of the politics of economic reform is built on the false premise that there is a neat correspondence between economic interest and political orientation. In reality, ideological, cultural and historical factors are just as important as structural ones in the determination of political alliances. This is particularly the case in Africa. Secondly, the political process is presented in terms of a 'real politic' in which people are motivated in terms of immediate material interests, so that policies to benefit the poor are only acceptable to the non-poor if the non-poor benefit too. The ultimate implication of this perspective is that the poor are effectively left with little independent initiative. At the local level, they are expected to operate within 'depoliticized' local communities concerned only with mobilising 'participation' in development. Local hierarchies of subordination and super-ordination, often germane to the incidence and perpetuation of poverty, are not problematized. At the national level, the demands of 'coalition politics' effectively subordinate the poor to the more politically articulate and resourceful non-poor. Within this vision, the poor remain effectively disenfranchised, their only 'freedom' being their ability to support reform programmes!

Mercifully, there are signs that this bleak scenario within reform thinking is changing, albeit slowly. Three important contributions in this regard are Salmen (1992), the *WDR* (1997) which focuses on the state, and the late 1999 speech by Wolfensohn at the Annual General Meeting of the Bank and the IMF. Beyond deploring the 'miracle of the market', Salmen argues that there is a need to empower the poor through strengthening their ability to articulate their specific demands:

> ...demand, particularly that of the poor, is inadequately understood and improperly linked to supply in development work. Because the poor have little purchasing power, they are peripheral to the structural market economy with which so much development thinking and activity is concerned. The demand of poor people for goods and services is tightly interwoven with their non-organisational institutions. Money alone cannot be used to demonstrate demand. The proper understanding of the poor's demands requires a sound assessment of institutional forces lying outside the formal market-place.... Effective demand is an extremely powerful source of information, incentive, and co-ordination. The ability of the poor to exercise it generally needs to be strengthened, and policies that might limit its effect should be approached with extreme caution (Salmen, 1992, 7–13).

The poor can be empowered by policies which deliberately seek to convert their often ignored demands into an effective 'voice'. To achieve this, he advocates a 'learning-process approach' to development work Specifically, he calls for beneficiary assessments in the preparation, design and implementation of projects. Institutional pluralism is considered crucial; the linkage between local organisations, communities and government agencies is emphasised (1992, 13). Importantly, Salmen points out that the development of local 'voice' is not enough. *Whose* voice is just as important. This brings local hierarchies into central focus as the disadvantages of power—not just that of economic capability—are problematized. He argues that institutional initiatives should reflect the nature of the problem on the ground. If the problem is the inattentiveness to the client's needs by development agencies, then the promotion of 'voice', incorporating both the poor and the non-poor might be sufficient. If, however, the problem is organisational overload, lack of clarity of goals or deep conflict about them, then the 'voice' option, incorporating heterogeneous local forces, might make things worse because of the tendency of the local elite to impose their own voice as the voice of the community. In such a situation, policy should seek to promote small groups, homogeneous enough to have a disciplined and relatively consensual goal-setting process. Within this vision, some initiative, and hopefully activism, is restored to the poor, particularly at the local level.

There have also been shifts in the way the state is conceptualised. Instead of the knee-jerk distrust of the state, a more nuanced approach is advocated in the *WDR* (1997) which looks at the role of the state in development. The agenda for the African state has moved beyond simply rolling it back and promoting electoral politics to include efforts at improving institutional efficiency by changing institutional behaviour within the state. Quoting Napoleon, the *WDR* (1997) reminds us that 'Men are powerless to secure the future; institutions alone fix the destinies of nations'. Public action through the state, long advocated by Dreze and Sen (1989), is brought back onto the agenda. However, the conception of politics and the state continues to be technocratic, managerial and electoral. The over-arching value is utilitarianism; a functioning, meritocratic technocracy will create the optimum conditions for market operations and efficiency. These will in turn lead to growth and reduced poverty. Solidaristic issues continue to be ignored.

The third suggestion of possible change in thinking can be gleaned from Wolfensohn's speech. He points out the crucial importance of 'good governance' for poverty alleviation world-wide. He notes that multilateral institutions are already spending huge sums of money annually on governance projects involving civil service reforms, budget management, tax administration, legal reform, judicial reform and institution building. Importantly, he 'also stressed the need to build a balance between macroeconomic and financial issues on one hand, and social and structural issues on the other (*Vanguard*, 30/9/99)'. This line of thinking, coupled with his support for debt relief and advocacy of a 'fair, comprehensive and inclusive' trading system should help to focus some attention on the external dimensions of low-growth and poverty in many African countries.

Reforms, rural reality and poverty

There is continuing controversy about the actual impact of the reforms in many parts of rural Africa. In Tanzania, for example, real GDP rose, on average, by 4 per cent with some increase in per capita income. However, it is also pointed out that shortcomings remain at the sectoral, household and firm levels. In rural

Tanzania, declining real farm incomes, increasing pressure on land, and opportunities created by economic liberalisation have given rise to a dynamic rural informal sector. This sector now employs about 21 per cent of the nation's labour force compared to only 7 per cent employed in the rural formal sector. Declining incomes and deagrarianization are unlikely to stem the tide of poverty.

In northern Nigeria, liberalisation has disrupted state-provided input supply systems without the market providing adequate alternative. Increases in the cost of production and subsistence far outstrip increases in the price of agricultural products, leading to a reproduction squeeze. There is increased internal differentiation in rural communities. Richer farmers continue to be able to attract a disproportionate share of the reduced support from the state. They also have the ability to delay sales till seasons of higher prices, and the ability to exploit far-flung markets, including lucrative cross-border parallel markets fuelled by currency differentials. They have generally done well under economic liberalisation. On the other hand, poorer farmers who constitute the majority of the rural population confront worsening conditions of production and reproduction. They produce less because of rising costs and they cannot provide the necessary capital to enable them to sell in the more profitable markets. In some village samples, up to 50 per cent of the households are net-deficit producers and they depend on bought food for varying periods of the year. Increased price of agricultural produce means that these net-deficit producers suffer from both production and reproduction pressures. Though some have adopted the strategy of income diversification, the urban informal sector, itself subject to reform pressures, has invaded the rural areas and has tended to depress incomes in the sector. The rural poor are often pushed into the most marginal of non-farm activities.

In south-western Nigeria where cocoa, an internationally tradable crop is the main crop, liberalisation brought considerable initial gains. But even under this relatively favourable condition, the situation of farm workers and female-headed households has worsened. Sharecroppers are forced to increase their contribution to production, whilst their share of the produce has remained constant. The youth, particularly from poor households, are increasingly forced into income diversification for want of land and the capacity to meet the rising cost of inputs. Even better off households are now facing severe problems. On the one hand, they face declining yields caused by ageing trees, exhausted soils and climatic oscillations. On the other, they face higher than average increases in the cost of chemical inputs and subsistence goods, and prohibitive costs for replanting their farms with higher-yielding varieties. International cocoa prices have declined since 1986 when the reform process started, putting some pressure on the local produce price. There is a huge stock of cocoa held internationally, and cocoa producers find it difficult to shore up world prices. The mortgaging of farms by hard-pressed farmers is becoming a prominent feature of rural life even in this region that has largely benefited from economic liberalisation. There is increased uncertainty in village life and conflict between farmers and traders is increasingly frequent. Cocoa farmers continue to plead for government support.

A central feature of these bleak rural situations is the over-determination of economic life by what is often a notional market. The market, as a regulatory institution, cannot just be willed into existence. Real markets take considerable time and effort to build up the trust and predictability which make them work. More often than not in rural Africa, state organisations plagued with ineffi-ciency were disbanded and replaced only by a notional market, particularly in resource poor regions or regions with poor transport facilities. And even where a factors and produce market has taken hold, social provisioning is governed by effective demand, rather than need. It may be argued that more people in rural areas are being drawn into remunerative employment through agricultural labour, and rural income diversification activities. But we must also pause to consider the real returns to this labour. Evidence abounds to suggest that: (a) extra-economic means of accessing labour are making a come-back in some places; (b) usurious forms of loan/wage relations are also being reactivated; (c) sharecroppers are being forced to increase their contributions to the production process. This is a recipe for increased misery. And some of the blame for the situation must lie squarely with the reform process itself.

These brief sketches make it possible for us to understand the progress of poverty in rural Africa in the 1980s and the 1990s despite programmes of eco-nomic reforms and poverty alleviation. Though the Bank estimates that the per centage of the population living in poverty in Sub-Saharan Africa will drop from 46 per cent of the total population in 1998 to 42 per cent in 2008, the abso-lute numbers will go up from 291 million to 330 million. In South Asia, how-ever, it is forecast that the per centage of the poor in the total population will drop from 40 per cent in 1998 to 14 per cent in 2008. In absolute terms, the numbers will drop from 522 million to 206 million (*World Bank,* 2000). Sub-Saha-ran Africa is one of the few regions in the world with a deteriorating poverty problem. The distribution of this poverty is likely to vary by country, region, and social group. If past trends are anything to go by, rural areas are likely to carry a disproportionate share. So will ecologically marginal areas like the Sahel. Women will be equally hard-hit.

Wider social indicators recently cited by K. Y. Amoako, Executive Secretary of the Economic Commission for Africa, and Peter Hain, British Minister of State for Africa in the Foreign and Commonwealth Office, paint a similar picture. In 1999, at least 30 per cent of Sub-Saharan Africa lacks access to medi-cal services, more than 40 per cent lacks access to safe drinking water. 25 per cent of children of school going age have no access to education; sixteen coun-tries have enrolment rates of less than 60 per cent. 20 per cent of the population is affected by civil wars and Africa now accounts for more than half of all war-related deaths in the world. 5,500 people are reportedly killed daily by AIDS, with life expectancy dropping in many countries (*APIC,* 12/10/99; *Guardian,*

17/10/99). The FAO's *The State of Food Insecurity in the World* suggests that in 1999 33 per cent of the children in Africa under five years of age were undernourished.

The *WDR* (1990, 140) predicts that Sub-Saharan Africa will need a growth rate of about 5.5 per cent a year to 'prevent the number of poor from increasing'. For his part, the Director of the Africa Division of the IMF, Goodall Gondwe, claims to be impressed by the performance of African economies in the period 1995–1998. The average rate of economic growth is put at 4 per cent a year. Inflation is said to have dropped from an aggregate 40 per cent in 1995 to 11 per cent in 1998. Projected growth for 1999 was put at 2.9 per cent (*Guardian*, 5/10/99). The situation remains critical as the benefits of the limited growth continue to eluded substantial sections of the population whose lives remain blighted by deprivation. Clearly the current reforms have failed to stem the tide of poverty and nothing can be gained by the mere assertion that things would have been worse without them. The challenge is to promote better and more balanced reforms through the 'genuine partnerships' advocated by Wolfensohn.

Conclusion: Poverty, power and institutions

The first lesson we must learn is that we cannot exclusively rely either on the operation of market forces, or on the state, or on the institutions of local communities (Dreze and Sen, 1989, 17). This wider sense of institutional pluralism can work only if we embrace the learning process approach and seriously privilege multiple local inputs into the design and implementation of policies aimed at economic reform and poverty alleviation. While this does not imply the abandonment of economic rationality, it certainly means that appropriate attention will also be paid to non-economic factors, particularly as expressed by the targets of the policies advocated. Beyond this, it will also be necessary to promote and encourage institutions of genuine public pressure in the reform of the African state. And these need not be limited to non-governmental organisations. Linguistic and cultural communities, trade unions, professional organisations and similar social groupings should also be encouraged to contribute positively to the direction of political and economic reform. Condemning such groups as parochial or 'tribal', or as self-interested 'vested interests' ignores their potential contributions.

At the root of the current problems of African countries lies the need to evolve political institutions which faithfully reflect and represent the views and interests of their constituencies while developing a solidaristic notion of the public good. War and ethnic strife have frequently resulted from the absence of such institutions. The character and structure of particular states, the moral tone of the leadership, and the latitude for public expression within them ought to condition the particular mix of policy. The state is not just a managerial force but also a representative and political force as well. The narrow concentration on managerialism limits the potential contribution of local communities to the reform process while the political emphasis on electoralism has already led to deformed patterns of democracy and the continuation of predatory practices in many African countries. Furthermore, changing institutional behaviour within the state will require much more than the money poured into governance projects. The livelihood of the bureaucrats, the cultural context of institutionali-sation, and the role of social forces in disciplining public institutions must all be taken into account.

Within this conception of the politics of economic reform, poverty eradica-tion depends critically on the ability of the poor to articulate their needs or organise themselves and create alliances with others to effect change in gov-ernment policy. Local activism should not be limited to the provision of a safety net. Unlike the presupposition inherent in the current reform process, local poli-tics, by communities, interest groups and individuals is central to the politics of economic reform and poverty alleviation. Politics is not only for the central state while the rural areas are confined to the sphere of administration. NGOs, both national and international, have been playing important roles in such fields as debt relief, emergency assistance, the defence of human rights, and poverty alleviation. But they are not a replacement for either the state, or for local com-munities. In too many cases, because they are seen as an alternative to the state, community-based organisations (CBOs) have been used to off-load the cost of reproduction of the population on women, particularly in the rural areas. The strengths and limitations of these intermediary organisations in any particular circumstance should be adequately taken into account in the formulation of pol-icy. The possibility that they may be serving interests other than the ones for which they are formed should be constantly kept in view.

Even when an appropriate mix is achieved between the market, the state, and public activism at the local, national and global levels, it will still be neces-sary to problematize the international context within which the development agenda is being pursued. The ways in which the structures and processes of the current globalization impinge on African life will determine the success or failure of many internal reform efforts.

References

APIC, 12/10/99, 'The African Development Forum—Dialogue for the African Renais-sance', Address by Dr. K. Y. Amoako.

Dethier, J.-J. (1999): 'Governance and Economic Performance: A Survey', Discussion Papers on Development Policy, No. 5, Centre for Development Research, Bonn University.

Dreze, J. and A. Sen (1989): *Hunger and Public Action*, Clarendon Press, Oxford.

Goyder, H. (1997): 'Poverty Reduction Strategies in Africa—measurement of effective-ness', ODI Indicators of Poverty Workshop, October 1997.

Hanmer, L., G. Pyatt & H. White (1997): *Poverty in Sub-Saharan Africa: What Can We Learn from the World Bank's Poverty Assessments?* Institute of Social Studies, The Hague.

Salmen, L.F. (1992): 'Reducing Poverty: An Institutional Perspective', Poverty and Social Policy Series, Paper No. 1, The World Bank, Washington, D.C.

The World Bank (1990): *World Development Report, Poverty.*

The World Bank (1997): *World Development Report, The State in a Changing World.*

The World Bank (2000): "Poverty Trends and Voices of the Poor.". www document, http://www.worldbank.org/poverty/data/trends/

The Guardian (Nigeria), 30/9/99, 'Mandela urges global war on poverty'.

The Guardian (Nigeria), 5/10/99, 'Africa's economic recovery impresses IMF'.

The Guardian (Nigeria), 17/10/99, 'Only Money Will Set Africa Free—Peter Hain'.

The Vanguard (Nigeria), 30/9/99, 'Debt relief, poverty alleviation, economic pillars of next century—World Bank boss'.

Chapter 5
The Institutional Heart of Rural Africa: An Issue Overlooked?

Kjell J. Havnevik

Introduction

This paper will introduce a journey on different paths that reflects my own experience of understanding, attained through field work, literature and discussions with colleagues primarily in Africa and the Nordic countries. The aim of the travelling has been and still is to search for a deeper understanding of the dynamics of agricultural and rural change in Sub-Saharan Africa—an understanding that might contribute to more relevant policies and interventions/support activities for enhancing rural African livelihoods. The aim of the journey is thus not unique, but similar to that of concerned institutions, including the International Fund for Agricultural Development, IFAD, researchers, policy makers and rural people.

Why is the understanding of rural African dynamics so important? Do not recent indicators show that Africa has overcome its crisis and recession; that for three consecutive years relatively high growth rates have been recorded in agricultural production and GDP? This may be so, but the sustainability of this trend is uncertain and parallel to this growth is a spreading and deepening of poverty. For example, statistics from Tanzania show that average annual agricultural growth has recovered to a level of about 5 per cent during the period 1993–1997, but at the same time rural poverty, i.e. the per centage of rural people living on less than one dollar a day, has increased from about 50 to 60 per cent. Similar tendencies occur throughout the region (refer to Mustapha in this volume and Wolfensohn, 1999).

These diverging trends between macro- and sectoral level statistics and increasing poverty on the ground have by some been referred to as "local noise", or as a disconnection between the macro- and micro-levels. Recent field studies from rural Tanzania (Morogoro and Songea) tend to confirm the local noise hypothesis in general by concluding that, "in liberalised Tanzania, farmers are farming more crops, risking more in marketing them, spending more and earning less" (Ponte, 1997). This research shows as well the interesting feature that farmers even in remote areas are induced by the need to generate more cash in response to increased commercialisation of rural life, to move to so-called "fast crops"—crops with shorter growing time that can fetch money in the markets. This and other recent studies indicate that the issue may not be lack of markets, but their organisation and functioning and what this implies for the relative power of the actors participating in them (Hårsmar, 1998).

The resilience of African poverty and its deepening and spreading with higher growth rates have become a major concern for all who are interested in justice and the well-being of African people. It is evident that it is simply insufficient or flawed to say, as Africa external institutions and agencies have tended to do for a long time, that higher growth rates should mainly be the centre piece to overcome the African poverty trap. The complexities of African rural dynamics require deeper insights to be understood properly, a finding also strongly conveyed by the recently concluded DARE programme, i.e. De-Agrarianisation and Rural Employment Research Programme (Bryceson, 1999). This Africa wide documentation and analysis shows that rural people are undertaking a delicate balancing act and succeeding to varying extents in clinging to livelihoods somewhere between and including farm and non-farm, family and individual and rural and urban activities. It is claimed by the programme that a process of de-peasantisation is ongoing in a context of tumultuous change and that poverty alleviation of rural target groups in donor projects is not sufficient to address the negative outcomes of this process.

This development is what has urged me to travel on different paths in search of a deeper understanding of the dynamics of rural and agricultural change in a broader context. For me, the journey is at present unfolding on the cultural path, reflecting the widening of the search to social, ethnic and cultural diversity with particular attention to the character and role of indigenous rural institutions. Before I go deeper into this, let me briefly introduce the various other paths.

The journey and its different paths

The economic path

The journey started about two decades ago and it was initiated by the concern that the economic reforms spreading throughout Africa did not sufficiently reflect the specifics of the African terrain. There was consequently a fear that it would not produce sustainable growth and contribute to meaningful livelihoods and instead generate increased indebtedness and high social costs and suffering. There was as well concern that the reforms did not build on a thorough understanding of the African nation building process, the role of the state, and the original trade-offs and "social contract" on which it rested (Olukoshi, 1998). The urge of African governments to create unity and consensus in the early phase of independence and combine them with economic modernisation were most often overlooked, in particular by external observers. This is among other things reflected in often repeated statements by international financial institutions and other agencies that since the mid-1960s until today the African economic situation has continuously deteriorated.

A more nuanced analysis shows, however, that the first stage of post-colonial African development, from around 1960–1973, saw very positive economic growth, which paralleled a positive global economic conjuncture, and which saw both an expansion of the state and rapid spread of health services and education. Even external donors and international financial institutions recognised and supported the important role of the African State. More constructive development took place in this period in many African countries than during the previous 60–70 years of colonial rule. What needs to be understood better is why the striving towards unity and modernisation, i.e. the post-colonial African development model, failed; why it could not be sustained and the role of foreign aid and external institutions and agencies in this process. My hypothesis is that the failure of the model related more to the adoption and enforcement of external and "alien" institutional set-ups, than has so far been accepted. A search in this direction might have led us onto the cultural and institutional path at an earlier stage.

The advent of the neo-liberal paradigm, which implied substitution of the state with the market as the driving force in development, Western co-ordination of their Third World policies and development assistance and the breakdown of the African post-colonial model opened for a new development era, i.e. that based on structural adjustment programmes (SAPs). It was over concern with this new agenda and its implications that the Nordic Africa Institute in co-operation with Sida in early 1987 convened a seminar on the topic, "The IMF and the World Bank in Africa; conditionalities, impact and alternatives" (Havnevik, 1987).

This was the period when the social consequences of SAPs were high on the international agenda and UNICEF had argued strongly for "adjustment with a human face". The Nordic countries had in the mid-1980s already notified the World Bank about their concern for the economic and social marginalisation and poverty associated with the SAPs and had requested the Bank to measure its spread and significance (Haxthausen, 1987, 173). The governments of the Nordic countries, however, did not put forward any concrete recommendations or ideas as to how to modify or change the SAP model so that it could address such effects in an integrated model. When Tanzania in November 1984 requested the Nordic countries to increase their support for its non-SAP based development strategy, the response was negative underlining that expanded Nordic support would be conditional on Tanzania signing an agreement with the IMF/WB for a stabilisation and comprehensive structural adjustment programme, which happened in August 1986.

What this background shows is that marginalisation and the spread of poverty in Africa have been a concern linked to the SAP reforms for a long time, and even prior to the reforms. As early as in 1973, Robert McNamara, the then president of the World Bank, in his famous Nairobi speech called for the redirection of the assistance of the Bank to target the poorest 40 per cent in the poorest countries (Gibbon, 1992). In addition the background shows the increasing unity with which rich and developed countries promoted and implemented their new development paradigm. Unlike the 1960s and 1970s, there was no back door entrance for the countries of the south to solicit increased assistance.

During the 1987 seminar we grappled as well with the question of owner-ship of the reforms and the interlinkages between the economic and political spheres in relation to SAPs. Although the focus was on the economic reform programmes per se and issues related to their foundation and relevance in the African context, the seminar could foresee that the political issues would come to be given a much more prominent role in relation to structural change in Africa in the future.

The political path

The interest in the political path started to grow among International Financial Institutions when they realised, although gradually, that African states were unable to establish "an enabling environment" for economic reforms, in particular in relation to legal, juridical and administrative frameworks that would be stable enough for the private sector to thrive. Hence the 1989 major World Bank report on Africa initiated the discussion of "governance", and in particular about the elements of what would be the type of governance that could help economic reforms to assist an economic take-off. The push for democratic reforms, i.e. changes in the political system, came somewhat later and was not driven by the World Bank, but by major Western countries and civil society institutions in Sub-Saharan African countries. The International Financial Institutions subsequently had to take this democratic conditionality on board.

During the 1990s, the multiparty political system emerged in most African countries—and led to an opening of a political space, but this space is in most countries controlled by the urban elite, and not by people in the rural areas who had only to a limited extent, at least outside some countries in western Africa, become organised. In addition, formal institutions dominated by the state are playing an important role in the political space.

The analysis of the sequencing of the economic- and political reforms and the potential and actual conflicts between them, have revealed that the agenda of international institutions and external agencies is not always in harmony with African people's aspirations and wish to decide on and themselves influ-ence the type of economic and political systems that they deem fit for their context. And as stated by Thandika Mkandawire, an African social scientist,

"Western countries were seen by many Africans to offer them democracy without choice" (Mkandawire, 1996).

There is another strand of research related to governance which goes deeper and relates to the character of the state and enhancement of democratic and human rights, that leads onto the third path, the research investigating and reflecting on social, ethnic and cultural diversity. This path in turn opened my eyes for the character and role of indigenous institutions; their role in influencing rural dynamics and for enhancing or obstructing meaningful livelihoods in the rural areas.

The cultural path; social, ethnic and cultural diversity

The social, ethnic and cultural diversity of Africa is unquestionable. For instance, of the world's about 6,000 languages nearly 2,000 are spoken in Africa. What is more debated is how this diversity has come about and the role it plays in contemporary development. Here the focus will be on the latter issue.

I will argue that elements related to the third path of the journey, social, ethnic and cultural diversity, are very important for guiding and influencing significant areas and processes of rural life and development. For instance they strongly influence the gendered division of labour, they are significant for control over and access to resources, they influence rules for natural resource management, they play an important role for reproduction, contribute to the maintenance of social security, and guide marriage and inheritance, in particular in rural areas. Often, the existence and significance of such indigenous institutions, controlled by the rural people themselves, or sections of them, are overlooked, particularly by external agencies and institutions with an objective to assist African rural development. The assistance approach thus easily puts emphasis on what new institutions have to be created or put in place in order for assistance to become effective and sustainable. This may not be a wrong approach, if it is based on acknowledgement and a deep understanding of the indigenous institutional pattern already in place on the ground.

As such this path, acknowledging its embeddedness in the rural society, influences rural production, access to assets, social relationships and rural life in the wider sense and consequently plays an important role for rural poverty issues. The social, ethnic and cultural features of this path constitute important elements of meaningful livelihoods in rural areas. On the other hand the mechanisms unfolding on this path are not necessarily non-discriminatory or non-exploitative. There is rich evidence that women have weaker rights, longer hours of labour and heavier work burdens than men (see Rwebangira in this volume). And furthermore there is ample evidence of exploitation and oppression in rural patron-client relationships. This implies that differentiation and power relations at local and community levels must not be overlooked in the quest for alleviating poverty (refer to Mustapha and Howe in this volume).

I will argue that the linkages and interconnections within and between the social, ethnic and cultural path and the wider society can be seen to constitute indigenous institutions that may obstruct or enhance processes of change. Depending on their character and density, social relations and networks may strengthen or weaken such institutions. Indigenous institutions in this context thus refer to systems, values and regulations that people apply to shape repeated human interactions. They build on elements from all paths, however, their distinctive character is that they have evolved through history from within African rural societies, i.e. they are culturally embedded.

The role of indigenous institutions in the African rural context has so far not played a dominant role in the international debate on development and poverty in Africa, although a number of researchers have addressed these issues for some time. The increasing acknowledgement, however, that the market based strategy is creating undesirable side-effects in rural Africa, such as the deepening of poverty, has created a space for looking anew at the institutional complexity of rural areas.

Maybe the best example of a possible desire for knowledge about this institutional complexity in the African rural context came from the World Bank official, who in a meeting at the Swedish International Development Agency, Sida, in Stockholm, on December 10 1996, stated that the World Bank's traditional approach to poverty reduction in Africa, i.e. investing in broad based growth, human capital and safety nets, had not worked in Africa. In rural Africa, according to him, there was a "black box", which the World Bank poverty division at that time did not understand. Evidently the World Bank representative was not fully aware that some of his colleagues in other departments of the Bank had already started the process of opening and investigating the contents of this "black box" (refer to Salmen 1992 and Narayan 1997).

I will argue that the "black box" can be seen to be constituted of indigenous institutions, and I will go on to outline in a broad perspective the content and implications of different theoretical positions on institutions in the African rural context.

But first, why is the institutional aspect so important in relation to market driven development, growth and poverty issues? Clearly institutional aspects are dynamically interlinked with the broader processes of societal change both of historic and contemporary character, including the recent ones emerging out of economic and political reforms. The nature of these dynamics is yet to be understood clearly. For instance, are indigenous institutions so vibrant and flexible that they can obstruct market driven development? Or, is the breakthrough for market based development in Africa held back because it has too little to offer the majority of rural people? Or, would a deepening of market penetration undermine indigenous institutions in such a way that increased economic growth necessarily would be accompanied by the spread of poverty? The analysis of rural indigenous institutions may thus offer important explanatory inputs for the understanding of the factors that constrain economic growth in Sub-Saharan Africa. The recent literature, strongly based on regression analyses, aiming at explaining the lagging growth in this region, has yet to provide satisfactory evidence (Havnevik and Hårsmar, 1999).

Theoretical positions linked to institutional aspects

At this point, two major and opposing positions can be discerned related to rural institutions in the African context. The second position can be broken down into three sub-categories. These positions (and sub-positions) can all be discussed in the context of factors hindering or obstructing development and the first category can be termed "constraints by lack of markets", the second "constraints by indigenous institutions" (the subsequent discussion builds on Hårsmar, 1998).

The constraints by lack of market position

The constraints by lack of markets position represents a widely shared view that lack of progress in SSA is related to the weak functioning of markets which has been undermined by an interventionist state apparatus. This, combined with lack of functioning factor and output markets, is significant in explaining the weak agricultural growth. Lack of infrastructure and indirect taxation further obstruct agricultural growth. According to this interpretation, smallholders are being "captured" by lack of functioning institutions. The World Bank and associated institutions have for a long time tried to understand better such an institutional context.

The constraints by indigenous institutions position

A growing share of the literature on Africa diverges from the above way of conceptualising the African rural context. The "constraints by indigenous institutions" literature builds on detailed historical case studies and contemporary field investigations. But within itself this literature differs in important respects as to interpretation of the institutional landscape and dynamics associated with rural change and poverty. A common point of departure for all these positions is, however, that rather than there being a dearth of institutions, they are widespread, and they function in a specific manner which obstructs or changes the directions of agricultural and rural development in certain ways.

(i) Fused power at local level
Maybe the most important representative of this position is Mahmood Mamdani, an African social scientist, who argues that colonial rulers in their launching of indirect rule brought about significant changes in the rural institutional context of Africa, changes that are still manifest. The basic idea about

indirect rule was to attain institutional and territorial segregation between the institutions and areas that served the colonial and the indigenous population. This system gave unprecedented power to the traditional chiefs who were able to usurp juridical, political and economic powers. Such powers were thus fused at the local level making it impossible for rural people to challenge them, unless through violent struggle, and on the other hand this effectively removed the chiefs' accountability to local people.

Post-colonial African countries dealt with the institutional legacy of the colonial regimes in different ways. But whatever way they responded to this legacy it created new problems. For instance, the conservative types of regime, Côte d'Ivoire and Kenya, deracialised the modern sector of their societies, but left the traditional, customary sector intact, and continued to base state post-colonial power on the fused power of local chiefs and traditions.

More radical regimes, such as Tanzania and Mozambique, tried to break the colonial legacy by instituting new institutional structures in the rural areas. But at the same time the single party political systems provided a foundation for increasingly authoritarian governments that created new divides between the urban and rural areas.

A preliminary reading of Mamdani, indicates that the problem is not lack of institutions in the rural areas, but on the other hand too strong institutions that in certain ways obstruct or channel agricultural development away from a process of accumulation from below (Mamdani, 1996).

(ii) Access through relations
Analysis of the interaction between the colonial regimes and traditional institutions is also the focus of much of the writing of Sara Berry, an American historian (Berry, 1993). She emphasises that the colonial administrations in Africa in their attempt to find an effective, low budget ruling system, seemed to have a firm belief that traditional communities consisted of mutually exclusive socio-cultural units with fixed customs, traditions and structures. Through their intention to uphold traditional norms and structures of authority, colonial officials were actually declaring their intention to build colonial rule on a foundation of conflict and change. Berry further shows that social relations have continued to be important channels for negotiating access to resources, in particular land, even in the post-colonial period. Thus such relations are also of vital importance for the poverty context. Her claim is that social relations and indigenous institutions are far from being stagnant and static, on the other hand they command flexibility in relation to both internal and external pressures and changes.

Others argue that Berry puts too little emphasis on power and structure, and too much emphasis on process as determining elements in the negotiations. The argument is that the strong have the power to define traditions and norms in their interest and thus shrink the space for negotiations (Amanor, 1999).

Numerous investigations and observations from rural Africa during the last two decades, show that smallholders to an increasing extent have been diversifying their income generating activities and investments both in productive assets and institutions. The reasons are seen to be the need to take advantage of new opportunities and responses to growing uncertainty in agricultural markets and the responses can be based on the need for survival, to reduce uncertainty, or to capture an additional profit or income, as among the more well-to-do (Bryceson, 1999 and Havnevik and Hårsmar, 1999).

(iii) Diversification as cultural characteristic

Another approach to understanding the dynamics of rural change is that emphasising the process of horizontal or lateral circulation of resources. The proponents of such a perspective, including Pekka Seppälä, attempt to develop a theory of smallholder diversification with such features that it can encompass the diversification of all social categories (Seppälä, 1998). Diversification is seen as a strategy through which to gain a special advantage by combining different activities and to stabilise the economic environment by net-working.

In the real context, segmented markets and the embeddedness of the economy in the cultural sphere create considerable spatial and temporal variations in prices. This leads in turn to difficulties in identifying real production costs for commodities and services. In this context accumulation occurs primarily when people take advantage of interfaces between different systems by converting value from one value frame to another. Thus diversification puts emphasis not so much on growth per se, but on the potential for horizontal and lateral circulation of value(s).

Reflections on the various theoretical positions

Different attempts have been made to classify the various theoretical positions as explanations for the weak development of agricultural and rural development in Sub-Saharan Africa. One line of inquiry or dimension is related to whether an institutional framework is seen to be present or not. The other is considering whether smallholders can be seen to act according to their own will, i.e. to what extent they are captured, or the degree of captivity.

On the first dimension, the two major positions stand clearly against each other; the World Bank arguing for the non-functioning of institutions, and Mamdani, Berry and Seppälä arguing for the existence of types of indigenous institutions albeit with different qualities. This emerges in particular when addressing the other dimension, that of degree of captivity.

The World Bank, although not employing the captivity concept, can be seen to refer to the problems of state intervention and interference with smallholders as a situation of captivity. With Mamdani it stands out clearly that smallholders are captured by strong, but "wrong", institutions as regards the potential for accumulation from below. Seppälä can be clearly put in the "uncaptured" position. With him the process of diversification is based on a theory that aims at explaining a process of behaviour that is selected and driven by the small-holders themselves. Berry falls rather into an intermediary position. On the one hand she discusses captivity by the state, on the other she criticises those who see smallholders as uncaptured by the state for not having seen how African governments have disrupted the livelihoods of rural people. On the issue of degree of captivity the analysis becomes complicated, and the problem is com-pounded by issues such as captivity of smallholders by whom and what, and whether captivity can be seen as a condition or hindrance to agricultural or rural development.

Hårsmar has tried to resolve this problem by arguing for the use of another type of distinction between the various positions, i.e. that of regulative and con-stitutive rules (Hårsmar, 1998). Guidance by regulative rules implies that people obey internalised societal rules that give reference to what is right or wrong, i.e. human behaviour is based on norm theory. To be guided by constitutive rules instead implies that people do things according to a common pattern because it makes sense to them, i.e. such rules inform people what is meaningful or not and the approach is based on more culturally oriented theory. On such a basis, a rough classification will place the World Bank, Mamdani and Berry in the "regulative rules guides behaviour" category and Seppälä in the constitutive one.

The analysis of the implications of the various theoretical positions means that the World Bank position sees market enhancing institutions as under-mining the hold of the state on smallholders. On the other hand Mamdani and Berry's perspective will mean that in spite of the World Bank being successful in this, smallholders will be constrained to enter market driven development due to the fused power context of the local, traditional structure. Seppälä would argue that smallholders would continue to act as they have done, as their common understanding is different from the market logic.

Conclusions

This paper's introduction to the various paths of a journey concerning the eco-nomic, political and cultural aspects of rural development, the presentation of their content, preliminary analysis and implications of the various rural institu-tional theoretical perspectives, thus argues for a further shift in the focus of investigation of rural dynamics and poverty in Africa in the direction of institu-tional cultural aspects. At the same time the paper indicates the problems and complexities associated with such a shift of emphasis of the research and knowledge focus.

So far the dominant strands of analyses related to nation building and struc-tural reforms have primarily been focusing on the economic or the political spheres or the interaction between them. When the focus of development shifts, which I think will occur, when consciousness and knowledge deepen, from the narrow perspective of economic growth to the broader one relating to support for meaningful livelihoods, the analysis must also become wider. With meaningful implying more than material aspects, and in particular the capacity for rural people to control and influence their own situation and future, the understanding and analysis must also incorporate more fully the cultural sphere, i.e. the social, ethnic and cultural diversity of rural Africa. The interesting focus for further understanding will then become the area where the economic, political and cultural paths overlap, and the objective must necessarily be to extend this overlap, to make it as large as possible.

References

Amanor, Kojo (1999): *Global Restructuring and Land Rights in Ghana: Forest, food chain, timber and rural livelihoods*. Research Report No. 108. Nordic Africa Institute, Uppsala.

Bryceson, Deborah F. (1999): "Sub-Saharan Africa Betwixt and Between: Rural Livelihood Practices and Policies" . ASC Working Paper 43/1999. Afrika Studiecentrum, Leiden.

Denninger, Mats, Kjell J. Havnevik and Marija Brdarski (1996): "Food Security in East and Southern Africa". Report presented to the Division of Natural Resources, Sida, Stockholm, chapter 3.

Gibbon, Peter (1992): "The World Bank and African Poverty 1973–91" . In *Journal of Modern African Studies*, Vol. 30 No. 2.

Havnevik, Kjell J. (ed.) (1987): *The IMF and the World Bank in Africa. Conditionality, Impact and Alternatives*. Seminar Proceedings No 18. Nordic Africa Institute, Uppsala, Sweden.

Havnevik, Kjell J. (1997): "The Land Question in Sub-Saharan Africa". In IDR Currents, December 1997. Department of Rural Development Studies, the Swedish University of Agricultural Sciences, Uppsala, Sweden, pp. 4–10.

Havnevik, Kjell J. and Mats Hårsmar (1999): "A Diversified Future—An Institutional Approach to Rural Development in Tanzania". EGDI paper. Swedish Foreign Ministry, Stockholm.

Haxthausen, Ulrich (1987): "Nordic View on the IMF/World Bank: Discussion". In Havnevik, K.J. (ed.), *The IMF and World Bank in Africa—Conditionalities, Impact and Alternatives*. Nordic Africa Institute, Seminar Proceedings No 18, pp. 173–5.

Jazairy, Idriss, Mohiuddin Alamgir and Theresa Panuccio (1994): *The State of World Rural Poverty. An Inquiry into Its Causes and Consequences*. Published for IFAD by the New York University Press, New York.

Mkandawire, Thandika (1996): "Economic Policy Making and the Consolidation of Democratic Institutions in Africa." In Kjell J. Havnevik and Brian van Arkadie: *Domination and Dialogue—Experiences and Prospects for African Development Cooperation*. Nordic Africa Institute, Uppsala, pp. 24–48.

Narayan, Deepa (1997): "Voices of the Poor—Poverty and Social Capital in Tanzania" . Environmentally and Socially Sustainable Development Studies and Monograph Series 20. World Bank, Washington D.C.

Olukoshi, Adebayo (1998): *The Elusive Prince of Denmark. Structural Adjustment and the Crisis of Governance in Africa*. Research Report No. 104. Nordic Africa Institute, Uppsala.

Platteau, Jean-Philippe (1996): "The Evolutionary Theory of Land Rights as Applied to Sub-Saharan Africa". In *Development and Change*, Vol. 27, Number 1, January 1996, pp. 29–87.

Ponte, Stefano (1997): "Get Your Cash Fast: Rural Households' Adaptations to Liberalized Agricultural Markets in Two Tanzanian Districts". Paper presented at the African Studies Association Meeting, Columbus, Ohio 13–16 November 1997.

Salmen, L.F. (1992): "Reducing Poverty: An Institutional Perspective". Poverty and Social Policy Service, Paper No. 1, The World Bank, Washington D.C.

Seppälä, Pekka (1998): *Diversification and Accumulation in Rural Tanzania*. Nordic Africa Institute, Uppsala, Sweden.

Wolfensohn, James D. (1999): "Coalition for Change". Annual Meeting Speech, IMF/World Bank Annual Meeting, September 28, Washington D.C.

World Bank (1997): *Rural Development. From Vision to Action. A Sector Strategy.* Environmentally and Socially Sustainable Development Studies and Monograph Series 12. Washington D.C.

World Bank (1998): "Growth and Peri-Urban Development in East Africa. A Concept Paper". DECVP. March 2.

Chapter 6
New Challenges and Opportunities in Smallholder Development in East and Southern Africa

Gary Howe

As we know, the idea of a changeless, essential Africa is a myth. Africa has had a very real history of change. For a certain period after the independence of many African countries, it appeared as though we could encapsulate Africa in a few rather static ideas. I believe that most of those ideas were incorrect even at the time. But recent transformations have been so dramatic even for the casual observer that we have no choice but to re-consider what we mean by rural development in Africa—what it involves and who the major protagonists are. I would like to offer a brief tour of some of the issues and opportunities that we are focusing on in IFAD as we try to come to terms with what poverty eradication actually means in the new context.

I would like to start by noting two extraordinarily important internal changes that hasten the potential to radically transform the profile of poverty eradication in Africa. One is economic liberalisation. The other is political liberalisation.

With regard to economic liberalisation I want to make one very basic point. It signifies that the period of government exploitation of the agricultural sector is coming to an end. State controlled prices that expropriated the value of agricultural output—especially of export crops—are on the way out. So are the artificial exchange rates and the foreign exchange controls that ensured that rural wealth was transferred to the urban minority. What this means is that farmers—and most African farmers are small farmers, smallholders—actually receive a larger share of the value they produce. In the past we used to talk about government savings and investment capacity and government sectoral plans. We still have to think about those. But the real issue of rural development is now the rate of smallholder savings and the framework for smallholder investment. It is a shift we all have wanted. But it also has tremendous implications for the real mechanisms of assistance to poverty eradication.

With regard to political liberalisation what we are really talking about is a process of deconstruction of the monolithic power of the central state apparatus. It means decentralisation. But perhaps much more importantly it means the opportunity for people—and especially the people without wealth and power—

to organise freely to pursue their social, economic and political interests. Just as in the economic sphere, the state is no longer so much at the organising centre of life. The issue of social organisation for poverty eradication is no longer an issue of state organisation but of the organisation of civil society—driven from below rather than from above.

We should not look at these two forms of liberalisation as separate and independent phenomena. The organisation and initiative of the poor will be essential to their economic development and their economic development will vastly strengthen their effective voice in the political process. If consolidated they represent a new and more positive framework for development that is not just responsive to the poor, but in some measure led by them. At the policy level we have to seek to guarantee achievements and promote further improvement. At the investment level we have to make sure that our assistance gets to the poor to ensure that they have the means to actually exploit these openings

The *first* set of problems involves market prices and competition. The good news is that farmers should be receiving a higher share of the international price of their products, particularly for export crops. The bad news is that market conditions are difficult. The most obvious point, but not one that we always keep in the front of our minds, is that the long-term trend in most mass agricultural commodity prices is downwards. Of course, annual fluctuations are often great but the general trend tends to be down. What it means is that African farmers have to produce more on a regular basis just to keep in the same place as far as income is concerned. Other parts of the world are not standing still. Africa confronts tremendous competition in the markets for its traditional agricultural exports, it has lost a huge part of its market, share in international trade in its traditional exports and the issue, therefore, is not only raising productivity, but raising it faster than its competitors.

At the small farmer level, liberalisation does not *necessarily* mean a prospect of continuing improved income from output. However, liberalisation very often *does* mean increased expenditures on inputs. If we take the case of Malawi as an example, the removal of transport subsidies for fertilisers has contributed to a very major price rise that has led to a collapse in the level of fertiliser use among small farmers. Similarly, the reorganisation of rural credit under the Malawi Rural Finance Company, which has the mandate to operate on a break-even basis, has led to a huge rise in interest rates—to approximately 35 per cent per annum. Taken together, the first effects of liberalisation have created a terrible crisis in the smallholder economy which is only mitigated statistically by the fact that most farmers were too poor to use credit and fertiliser even before liberalisation. Some producers are benefiting, but not most of the poor. The challenge in front of us is to work out ways to help put the poor in the line of those who have benefited and we are not at all sure that this will happen auto-matically through the operation of market forces. That is really the crux of the matter—we cannot subscribe to the belief that all things work themselves out to the good, at least for the good of the poor.

The *second* set of issues relates to Africa's relations to the international system of capital mobilisation and investment.

The current process of globalization expresses, in part, huge international flows of capital allowing some developing countries to make great leaps in productivity and income. These flows have given rise in some areas to major crises as in Asia during the second half of the 1990s. But there can be no doubt that international flows of capital to some developed countries have tremendously accelerated growth and poverty reduction. A very basic point that has to be made about this capital flow to developing countries is that it has involved private capital. The significance of public development assistance in overall capital flows to developing countries has been dwarfed by private investment.

Sub-Saharan Africa has been very unsuccessful in capturing part of this new wave of private investment in developing countries especially in the rural sector. Moreover, the real volume of international *public* assistance to smallholder development in Africa has been *declining*. Overall Africa has not benefited from the new wave of globalization of investment. I believe that this has serious potential consequences for poverty eradication. Major investments will be necessary to establish African smallholder agriculture and rural production on a competitive footing. So far Africa has not been able to establish the links to international capital that have impelled productivity and income rises in many other areas.

The *third* set of issues involves the political situation. Obviously, it is absurd to talk about political liberalisation in the too many cases of open conflict and civil war. But there are also cases of important countries not least in East and Southern Africa where it is extremely difficult to argue for the reality of substantial change. Greater control by the poor is not the same as formal democratisation. This control is created by organisation, by capacity to articulate interests and pursue them. In many cases that capacity does not yet exist. The failure to develop it will be just as consequential as the lack of linkage to investment capital. It will disarm the poor at a moment in which international production and wealth is being redistributed on the basis of the capacity to organise the productive process and to mobilise investment.

I would like to briefly take stock of the situation. There are important and positive internal changes taking place in Africa that strongly favour at least in principle savings and investment by the poor, and political and organisational development to serve their interests. But, there are serious gaps in the ability of the poor to capitalise upon these changes—and the international economic environment is posing severe competitive and price challenges that are being responded to without much assistance from major public investors.

If we are to, materially, contribute to overcoming these challenges and put poverty eradication on a dynamic economic and social footing we have to keep uppermost in our minds some basic points:

First, no sustained poverty eradication is possible unless it is built upon increased production by the poor—and institutions effectively serving the poor that are economically and financially sustainable in the new context of articulation between international, national and local prices. It is entirely wrong to believe that the poor because they are poor somehow live in a parallel and unconnected economy. When devaluation in Ghana sent the price of fertilisers sky-rocketing our carefully crafted programme of credit for input-intensive maize production collapsed as farmers realised that the change in price relations necessitated a major shift in their own investment and production strategies. What became very clear was that the macroeconomic shift required us and the farmers to re-think our development strategies involving not least a shift in our thinking about what is the appropriate focus for smallholder production. Our attention was very much drawn to the issue of *profitability* and *cash flow*. Farmers need more cash to meet new prices for inputs, and that makes us think much more about competitive position and comparative advantage. Inevitably this has meant that we have had to review the viability of development based on established crops and has impelled a much more active search for opportunities for crop and activity diversification. Yes, we are looking for social benefits but these will not materialise unless we reach a competitive level of productivity among the poor.

Less often understood is that service institutions themselves must also be financially and economically sustainable. Institutions must have an adequate revenue source and they must cover their real costs. This was not an issue in the past in relation to many public sector agencies including agencies providing economic services. The privatisation of many services and the tenuous financial basis of many public agencies have put cost coverage at the top of the sustainability agenda. This means that the positive cash flow of the poor has to be *increased* if the same effective level of services is to be assured.

Second, what is financially and economically sustainable varies enormously both *among* regions and *within* communities. As we move to a situation in which real costs are levied for work and services, we have to accept that production and institutions in different economic conditions will have to change in different directions to respond to the imperative of cost coverage. If resources are to be used well they must reflect underlying economic advantages. We do no good to the poor if we try to lead a counterfactual process on the basis of social equity. The point is not always equal and identical development, but positive change everywhere.

Let me give an example. In marginal and isolated areas, response to fertiliser application is low but fertiliser costs are high (because of transport charges). In higher potential areas, the physical response is higher and costs are lower (because of a higher level of development of communications. Now it is very clear that the sustainable development strategies for these two types of situation are very different. The lower potential areas should de-emphasise intensification of production and limit market orientation. By contrast the higher potential area might well be better served by pursuing a high input, market oriented production strategy. This has important institutional development implications: in the loss potential area, the focus may well be on using local resources better (for example, through a focus on soil and water conservation) involving a premium on community and individual natural resource management; in the high potential area, the focus may well be on strengthening market linkages and access to credit which may involve an emphasis on the development of commercial services.

There is no longer, if there ever was, any single appropriate production or institutional development model. But the issue is not restricted to increasing differentiation among regions or zones. It is also a question of differentiation within communities. We have often talked about the African community as though it were somehow homogeneous. We know that this is not really true, but the language we use does not reflect this very well. Now we also should realise that social and economic differences within communities will increase as the liberalisation process takes hold. Different sub-groups, with different assets, will have different opportunities and different constraints. I believe that if we are serious about building poverty eradication upon firm economic foundations we have to recognise this differentiation—and capitalise upon it.

One of our principal concerns is the situation of rural women. When we talked about mainstreaming women in development in the past, it was often assumed that this meant bringing them into the "main" development path. I think that as the rural world evolves there will not be one development path, but many. Just as pursuing poverty eradication means a general re-thinking of rural development strategies with an eye on the comparative advantage, actual or potential, of small producers, we have to ask, for example, whether the agricultural production path is always going to be the most effective one for income generation and food security among rural women or if the evolution of the rural economy is not offering new and different opportunities more consistent with women's real opportunities and assets. In some cases, for example, would it not be better for women to be empowered to pursue opportunities in the burgeoning rural non-farm economy gaining food security through income generation rather than on-farm food production? While this appears a simple question it touches on some very delicate issues; on the assumed primacy of agriculture as the major path of rural poverty eradication—and on direct production of food as the main avenue to food security. The point is that we have to help different groups do what they do best, leaving behind the idea that true progress is homogenisation. The critical question is in *which* production and market niche does each group have the strongest assets—and how we can strengthen that particular comparative advantage.

Third, there is an absolute economic imperative to support the local level organisation of the poor. The point is not only democratisation and participation as ideals but the simple fact that if investment and organisational initiative are now increasingly in the hands of the rural poor and smallholders—then it should be with the poor rather than the state that the planning process starts. If greater productivity and income among the poor require a higher level of economic services and linkage with the world outside the community then we should not be looking to government (which has no capacity)—nor to the private sector which has shown no or little interest. The poor have to look to themselves through traditional and new structures. And we have to help them.

Fourth, local level participatory development is essential but it is not always enough. Remembering the need for producers of all sorts, including smallholders, to strengthen their competitive position, we should recognise that in some cases they still need significant access to investment capital, to efficient processing and handling facilities, and to new technology. Notwithstanding the weak penetration of a sophisticated private sector in smallholder areas, it is essential to attract the private sector, national and international, into the process of smallholder development as interested parties, not as benefactors. The issue is one of linkage: how we can help facilitate connections between small producers and large investors and service providers—and how this linkage can serve the interests of both sides.

I would like to turn now to how IFAD has come to address these issues. Traditionally IFAD has been very cautious about cash crop development partly because of the emphasis on food security and partly because of the very poor terms of trade in cash crops for much of IFAD's operational history in the region. We still maintain a strong emphasis on the production of food crops not least because of their particular importance for women. However, we and many African farmers have reservations about the long-term possibility of income growth on the basis of coarse cereal grain production under smallholder conditions. Increasingly we have focused on providing the option of development in cash crops or higher value food crops where there is a certain comparative advantage in local production for the market.

I should say immediately that this is not a top down modification of our strategy. In Hoima and Kibaale Districts in Uganda a very intensive process of consultation with poor farmers has led to a major emphasis on access to improved banana and coffee planting materials as well as on market access roads, the IFAD projects' second phase. Also in response to demand, we are helping to introduce better performing cassava planting material to meet basic food requirements but it is very clear that farmers want access to cash as well as food not least to support the local services that are being improved on a cost recovery basis. In line with the need to establish new lines of responsive service supply, the producers of new planting material will not be Government, but medium-scale private operators.

What is most striking in our recent experience is not that farmers are increasingly oriented to the market, but what has to be done to establish a competitive and profitable position. Over the last few years we have developed small scale irrigation projects or programmes in Kenya (2), Zambia, Zimbabwe, Malawi and Ethiopia—with irrigation also representing important elements of projects in Tanzania, Madagascar and Eritrea.

What this reflects is the fact that we find it increasingly necessary to search out opportunities for diversification *out* of traditional food crops to establish smallholders in an activity with reasonable prospects for growth and income generation. Again, this is not to suggest that we are starting to abandon food crop production but that when we try to address cash generation we increasingly have to facilitate change. That change very often involves moving smallholder production onto a different level of technology and capitalisation. Making smallholders more competitive will very often involve considerably increasing the level of farm investment. We can make this change more accessible to the poor through much more cost-conscious approaches to capital development drawing upon local techniques, materials and skills—as well as the inputs of self-organised farmers. But it is still a very major change.

Just how important farmer organisation and mobilisation are for allowing the poor to have access to competition-enhancing technology and infrastructure has been brought home to us in our Marginal Areas Project in Tanzania. The project started many years ago within the framework of a top down and input intensive approach. The smallscale irrigation installed was very expensive and suffered major problems of management and maintenance. By mid-term we had achieved low penetration and poor yields. Following a very critical internal review, the orientation was changed dramatically towards farmer identification and management of schemes, and increased local inputs into the construction process (a process which we supported by helping expand local construction capacity through training local masons, for example). The result is that development costs have plummeted (from over $9,000 to less than $800 per hectare), maintenance problems have virtually disappeared, the number of smallholders involved has multiplied, and yields have risen consistently. Similar approaches are being pursued in Malawi and Zimbabwe, where we have successfully worked with government to have this adopted as the core of national irrigation programmes, and in Tanzania we are about to prepare a new programme expanding the approach that has been developed with farmers on a much larger scale. Given the Nordic scope of this seminar I am very happy to recognise that this approach to small scale irrigation through national programmes has been developed in the closest possible operational collaboration with DANIDA in a relationship that we consider a model for cooperation with bilaterals in the region.

I am presenting this not as an example of our success (and the success of our partners), but to make three points: that poverty eradication in a liberalised economy can require important investments, that the organisation of the poor can contribute to reducing the cost of investment and expanding accessibility; and that such investment can be highly profitable. The last point is extremely important. Our job is to show that positioning small farmers in more profitable lines of activity not only reduces poverty but is a commercially attractive proposition for the private sector at all levels, and that this sort of transformation can be integrated into a largely independent dynamic or private sector development.

This is not to suggest that intensive investment is the sole solution to poverty and food insecurity. Far from it. IFAD has historically been oriented to marginal areas, especially under its Special Programme for Sub-Saharan Countries Affected by Drought and Desertification and in many of these areas there are very few opportunities for high input market developments. Our strategy for these areas is quite different. First, we have stepped back from production development through major input use. Put simply, what might have been possible under pan-territorial uniform pricing is no longer economically or financially viable. Second, we have moved forward to explore how external inputs could be replaced by better utilisation of existing local human and natural resources. In these areas, the centre of attention has been on resource conservation rather than input use particularly within the framework of community resource management.

However, I believe that it is very important to recognise that marginal areas are not exempt from the increasing need to make all interventions financially and economically viable at the local level. I think the consensus now is that we are unlikely to have much success in establishing a broad-based farmer-led process of investment in conservation unless we can demonstrate approaches that are sufficiently cheap and productive to attract the farmer's own resources. I believe that quite a lot of progress has been made in this area particularly in water harvesting and pit-based cultivation in Burkina Faso and Niger, where we have long-running national programmes but there is a constant temptation to fall back to subsidy-based approaches masquerading as incentive programmes, approaches which are unlikely to be sustainable, and which actually block the development of strategies attuned to the underlying economics of marginal farm operations.

The lesson of this is not that it takes a lot of money to eradicate poverty but that in some places it makes a big and sustainable difference and in some places it does not. In helping African farmers reposition themselves in the global economy with a limited amount of seed capital, that is a crucial lesson to learn and use. But the issue of different development paths is not just about different agro-ecological zones. It is also about different groups even within the same community.

Taking up, again, the question of gender, we in IFAD, like many others, felt that gender sensitivity meant making sure that women had access to the same production activities, resources and institutions as men. That is still a very important aspect of our operations. But closely scrutinised field experience is leading us to think that this is not the whole story. When we review, for example, what women use rural credit for we find that they are not typically using credit to invest in crop production. They use it for a wide range of non-agricultural, fast turnover activities very much oriented to the market such as trading, smallscale agro-processing, and a wide range of services.

Now women represent a large per centage of the rural poor and we have to help to position them in more sustainably profitable economic roles. It has rather strongly occurred to us that we should be building upon what women are already choosing, that we should be supporting their development in a line of activity that is typically different from what men do but which very much reflects, for example, specific aspects of the real world of the volume and timing of female labour availability. Non-agricultural operations are emerging as an important line of activity which we are trying to explore in a way that recognises that it is very often women who predominate in these activities. Our first important investment in this area is in a micro-enterprise project for Rwanda. We expect much more of this as we start to use a recently approved Norwegian grant that will enable us to more actively experiment with concrete and differentiated strategies for responding to women's particular opportunities for income generation in a context of increasing cash income and exchange.

I suspect that this attempt to support women's own strategies for income maximisation in a changing economy will lead to a reappraisal of what "women in development" means. The fact that women in the African smallholder economy are responsible for a very high per centage of food production does not necessarily mean that this will be their niche for the indefinite future.

I would also like to quite briefly reflect upon the assumption that the best road for women is to integrate them into gender-independent institutions. Truthfully, it seems that this approach can involve very major pitfalls as in Uganda, where we have been really listening hard to what local people want. Here women prefer to run their own credit institutions which, incidentally, are doing very well, indeed. The explanation is that they fear that organisations that mix men and women will inevitably be dominated by men in a situation in which men and women have different economic interests and activities. What this suggests to us is that in some contexts, not only do we have to see a necessary differentiation in promising lines of activities for men and women, but we may also encounter the need for them to be organised in separate institutions. Again, this is not a theoretical position, it reflects the voice from the field.

This issue of the voice from the field leads me to the question of how planning has to change to reflect a farmer-led rural investment process. I believe that we all should recognise that when governments were in the investment and service supply seat our activities reflected the structure of government ministries rather than the livelihood strategies of the poor. We have to change radically if we expect farmers' organisations to play a critical role in gearing up to the competitive challenge. In early 1998 I had a conversation with the Minister of Agriculture of a small country in the Horn of Africa. The Minister asked me to arrange for an IFAD financed livestock project—to which my answer was that IFAD does not "do" projects for livestock, it does projects for people. Now the point here is that what the Minister suggested is very much in line what has been done in the past. We have, in fact, "done" irrigation, livestock and credit projects in which we simply assumed that the people involved organised their lives on such sectoral lines and that they just happened to agree with the definition of their problems as specified by a technical subsectoral department in the capital. This approach virtually guaranteed a low level of participation, and a consistent underdevelopment of the role of community and group organisation in the development process.

This approach has been more or less abandoned in IFAD. Our position is:

1. that every proposed project or programme must be preceded by a socioeconomic study or participatory rural appraisal;
2. that these activities both identify major groups of the rural poor (and their major interests) and the organisations that represent them; and,
3. that the process of identification of project objectives and activities be developed with the active participation of those groups.

Our final answer to the Minister therefore, was that while we were unwilling to commit ourselves to a livestock project, we were very willing to start a process of local consultation to identify local needs and interests and that if this involved livestock we would be happy to finance livestock support operations, but only in the direction of the priority concerns of the target groups and with the target groups' active participation. However, this sort of approach to demand based programme development is only part of the story. It has to be accompanied by assistance to capacity development to ensure that demand is articulated and listened to throughout the period of project implementation and beyond. As we move towards a farmer-led and farmer-executed investment process, our own activities have to shift from hardware to software and specifically towards strengthening the capacity of the poor to express their demands and organise the response, not only with regard to the mobilisation of their own resources, but also, and this is critical in many contexts, with regard to establishing an equitable interface with up-stream institutions both public and private. Competition requires services and many of these are going to have to be organised by farmers themselves. This will not happen unless we listen to their voice and strengthen their capacities.

This leads me to the final issue that I want to address before concluding: the relation between smallholder development and the private sector, including the large scale private sector. Here I want to refer to experiences in a particular country—Uganda.

IFAD's strategy in Uganda has been to increasingly accompany food crop support with assistance to smallholders in cash crop development. In particular, we have invested heavily in smallholder cotton production in the area north of Lake Kyoga, and we are just launching a programme to support edible oil production, palm oil in the south and southwest, sunflower oil in the north. Small farmers want cash, and these seem to us and to the farmers viable lines of development. But it became very clear to us that smallholder development could not take place only on the basis of the farmers themselves. The small farmer product required processing and, in the case of cotton and palm oil, that processing could not be done economically or competitively on a small scale. However, it was also evident that government could not play a direct role in the processing industry.

Faced with the imperative to establish access to advanced processing services if the Ugandan smallholder product was to be price competitive, our response has been to involve large private investors. An integral part of our cotton rehabilitation programmes in which we are in full partnership with the World Bank, is the revival of' the cotton ginning industry through privatisation of the cotton ginneries. In the palm oil activity, we are co-operating with government in the mobilisation of private investment in medium-scale oil extraction mills. The point is that in neither case could smallholder exploitation of an important opportunity take place without association with the private sector.

We have two major objectives in Uganda:

First, we want to demonstrate the mutual profitability to smallholders and the private sector of this sort of association. This demonstration effect is very important in Africa. For very good reasons this sort of investment withered away for a long time, and it is essential that it be proven to be viable in an area where private investors have long been extremely wary of large and long-term commitments.

Second, and I believe this to be an absolutely crucial role for those concerned with long-term poverty eradication, we have a role in helping ensure that the benefits of association are reaped by the poor through assistance to the development of the organisations and institutions that give the poor bargaining power in their relations with organised large scale capital. In the case of oil palm, for example, a major focus of our activities is strengthening the smallholder growers associations and the joint smallholder-processors industry body. Association of smallholder activities with private investment has perils as well as advantages for poverty reduction, and I believe that the right sort of external assistance can help ensure through the social organisation of the poor themselves that the benefits outweigh the costs.

We believe not only that there are structural changes ongoing in Africa, but that smallholders are fully aware of them and are seeking to exploit the advantages and defend themselves against the threats. If they succeed poverty will be reduced. If they fail poverty will get even worse. I believe that we now understand in general terms the need to pursue comparative advantages to the hilt; to accept and even embrace the need for economic and institutional differentiation; to forge alliances with the private sector, and to strongly support the participatory organisation to play roles that nobody else will but which are essential not only to link the poor to the larger economy, but to secure them better terms. Not only do we understand these things in general terms, but organisations like IFAD with a long history of coming to terms with rural poverty also have accumulated experience in putting what we know to work.

In closing I would like to remind you that the secret history of modern production is *capital*, and I would invite you to reflect on two priorities in East and Southern Africa. *First*, we have to confront the need for the re-establishment of functioning rural finance systems. Development needs investment. The work that IFAD and others are doing with local savings and credit institutions is important in local resource mobilisation. But we also need to forge linkages between local institutions and up-stream financial institutions to allow the inflow of funds on commercial terms—necessary to reposition and re-tool smallholder agriculture. *Second*, we have to think and act very seriously about accelerating the inflow of private investment in rural areas and helping organise the social framework in which the poor are not victims but partners. I would invite you to join with us in addressing these issues not in theory but in practice.

We can make a real difference. We know the challenges. We also know many of the *answers*. The point is no longer to describe the situation, but to change it. I hope that this meeting, and others to follow, will contribute not only to our knowledge of the problem, but to the further development of our joint action to do something about it in a way that reflects the need not only for greater co-ordination among UN agencies, but among all of us with the same objectives but individually limited resources to pursue them.

Chapter 7
The Legal Status of Women and Poverty in Africa with Special Reference to Tanzania

Magdalena Rwebangira

Introduction

This chapter looks at the legal status of women and its implications for poverty in Africa, drawing on Tanzania as a case study. The paper is divided into five parts. Part Two gives an overview of the legal status of women in Africa, taking constitutions, family and property laws pertaining to productive resources such as land, livestock and credit as the laws providing the framework for women's status and poverty. Part Three looks at the legal changes that have taken place in some of the African countries and reviews them as to the extent of their possible impact on poverty among women. Part Four takes Tanzania as a case study and looks at how efforts aimed at poverty eradication and/or alleviation may be hampered by the low status of women. The summary and conclusion are in Part Five.

Overview of the legal status of women in Africa

All laws whether formal or informal reinforce each other and form an environment which ultimately may determine whether a particular programme, policy or plan will succeed or not. However, for the purposes of this paper laws taken to have a direct impact on poverty are constitutions, family laws and property laws relating to access to productive resources such as land, credit, livestock etc.

In almost all African countries women are discriminated in some way under national constitutions, family laws and especially the customary and religious laws and traditional practices. Moreover, this situation is exacerbated by a pluralistic legal system characteristic of former colonies whereby modern statutory laws operate side by side with religious and customary laws. Consequently, many legal initiatives are not as effective as intended. Moreover, they are often not sufficiently focused to have a meaningful impact on women's poverty.

Let us begin with national constitutions. Ten years ago hardly any African constitutions had gender as a prohibited basis of discrimination. Thus the new African nation states proceeded under the assumption that women were second class citizens, although the trend was changing in many countries around the world.

As for family laws, in Ethiopia the Civil Code of the Empire of Ethiopia, 1960, provided a uniform legal code governing all personal matters such as marriage, divorce and adoption. It also outlawed all customary laws pertaining to these matters. Yet although this progressive Code has been in operation for almost four decades, its operation has been hampered by two problems. One is the status and prevalence of customary practice and another is women's inability to control and manage matrimonial and household property. Both issues hinder the alleviation of poverty among women.

After independence, Tanzania pioneered with its Law of Marriage Act (LMA), 1971 which was ironically based on Kenya's 1969 White Paper on Marriage and Divorce. This law provided for a minimum age for marriage. This aimed at discouraging early marriage of girls to give them time to get an education, mature and acquire the skills they need before marriage. It also gave women important property rights during and after marriage including division of matrimonial assets on dissolution of marriage. Nonetheless, the court in arriving at a decision on these matters, as well as child custody, was enjoined "to give due regard to the customs of the community to which the parties belong". However, the LMA categorically stated that customary and Islamic Laws pertaining to these matters had been superseded. Similar family law reforms were instituted in Mozambique after FRELIMO's victory in 1975 and positive gains were registered by women before they were torn down by the cold war inspired civil conflict.

In Zimbabwe, the Legal Age of Majority Act, 1982 gave Zimbabwean women of African origin full legal capacity at the age of 18 for the first time. This meant that among other things, women could acquire and dispose of property without the assistance of their fathers, husbands, brothers or other guardians as was hitherto the case under customary law. They could also inherit intestate from their fathers. However, the latter right can only be exercised if there are no sons. Access, ownership and control of land in Zimbabwe is governed by the Communal Lands Act, Cap. 204. Land falling under communal land tenure is vested in the chief on behalf of his followers. All people therefore have usufruct rights but primary rights of usufruct go to married men. Allocation of new fields to a man marks the beginning of an independent household with him as its head. Although District Councils have authority to grant occupation and use permits to any person not having vested rights to occupy land, the councils are enjoined to "give regard to the custom pertaining to the allocation and occupation of land in use in the area concerned". Consequently, District Councils allocate land in terms of customary law, which means that women are excluded from all land allocation.

Consequently, in many of these and other African countries, these legislative and policy changes did not go far enough to strengthen women's legal status in the light of negative customs (both authentic and neo-colonial) invented by colonialists in connivance with male elders. This situation continues to undermine African women's legal status today. Religion, especially Islam, which stipulates parallel provisions in family law and succession has been a source conflict of law if not political will in practice.

Laws relating to productive resources such as land, livestock and credit are often supposedly gender neutral although their application is invariably gender specific. At the time of the scramble for Africa, clans and families wanted to keep their land within their entity. Thus they did not allocate it to women who were expected to get married and move away from the family settlement. Thus land was allocated to men. While in almost all African countries women had relative control over the proceeds of their labour in pre-colonial days, the European land tenure system introduced by the colonisers handed over the fruits of women's labour to men either as husbands and therefore heads of households or as owners of registered land where individual titling and registration extended to communal lands as was the case in Kenya. Where land remained in the realm of customary land tenure the recognition of heads of households as owners of land worked to the disadvantage of women. Moreover, attempts at modernising, albeit from above, of rural agricultural communities such as Tanzania's Villagisation Programme of the mid 1970s also fell in the same trap.

Thus even in these countries where there were attempts at modifying family and property laws to meet new demands, inheritance laws especially related to land continued to exclude women. Women could only access land through fathers, husbands and sons. Divorced and widowed women were denied both social and economic space for an autonomous existence.

Legal changes in the last fifteen years

During the last fifteen years, the 3rd UN World Conference on Women in Nairobi 1985, the UN Human Rights Conference in 1993, the International Conference on Population and Development in 1994 (Cairo), the Social Summit held in Copenhagen in 1994 and particularly the 4th UN Conference of Women held in Beijing in 1995 have helped in various ways to put gender on the agenda in Africa, as elsewhere.

These international platforms were important for African women in many ways. Firstly, many NGOs, CBOs and individual African women and activist groups participated in them, enabling them to relate issues to their own platforms at home. Secondly, even for the many African women who did not participate in any of them, it was heartening to know that the world now focused on women every once in a while. As one woman is reported to have said when the 1985 Nairobi Conference closed for the day to see women at work, "if all these people have come to Kenya from around the world just to talk about women, I must be important. No matter what my husband says" (Gachukia, 1991).

Coincidentally, this period has witnessed the end of the cold war, acceptance of political pluralism in principle, trade liberalisation and the dawning of a new era of democratisation in Africa. Other factors have been the fall of racist regimes and apartheid in Zimbabwe, Namibia, South Africa and the fascist regime in Uganda. The wind of change is blowing across Africa.

Consequently, almost all African countries have ratified the Convention on the Elimination of All Forms of Discrimination against Women (CEDAW) during this period. Furthermore a number of sub-regional organisations such as SADC, and COMESA have adopted gender profiles. Moreover, the gender based civil society at grassroots, national and regional levels has been strengthened in the knowledge that they are fighting for a just cause and they are not doing so alone. They have networks around the globe and more recently within Africa itself.

The Declaration by Heads of States or Governments of the Southern African Development Community (SADC) made at Blantyre, Malawi on 8 September 1997 made a commitment among others, to promote women's full access to, and control over productive resources such as land, livestock, markets, credit, modern technology, formal employment, and a good quality of life in order to reduce the level of poverty among women (SADC Declaration paragraph H3).

Nonetheless, despite the euphoria that accompanies this environment, there is still a general lack of focus to address root causes of poverty among women, their families, communities and indeed African nations. This is surprising when one considers that poverty is the number one critical area of concern for the African Platform of Action as well as for the Beijing Platform. African governments worked hard to include poverty as a global critical area of concern. As commented by Sherif Omar Hassan in his key note address to the Gender and Law Conference in Addis Ababa in October, 1997, *"The feminization of poverty is a consequence of women's unequal access to economic opportunities"*. This paper goes further to suggest that the stagnation and lack of momentum in the economies of African countries are to a significant extent due to their leaders' persistent disregard of their women, whose sector (agriculture) is the backbone of the African economies.

Yet, we have recently witnessed new legislative moves to strengthen the status of women in some African countries. The national constitutions of Uganda, Ethiopia, Eritrea and South Africa prohibit sex as a basis of discrimination. Among these the constitutions of Uganda and South Africa stand out. The Ugandan Constitution recognises the right of both men and women to enjoy equal rights in marriage, equal responsibility in bringing up the offspring of marriage and outlaws customs and traditions that undermine the status of women and their health. Furthermore, it calls for protection of the family as the basic unit of society. It also guarantees women's participation in decision making.

This is different from Kenya, Tanzania, Zambia, Zimbabwe, Lesotho and Namibia, where sex is still permitted as a basis of discrimination under the national constitution. The Constitution of Kenya, in particular, recognises the application of customary and religious laws "to the exclusion of any other laws".

Moreover, the 1990s have witnessed additional bold steps in both legislation and policy initiatives in some African countries. In Zimbabwe, for example, the Deed Registries Amendment Act No. 2 of 1991 removed the married women's previous disability to register immovable property in her name without her husband's assistance or proof of his permission. The Finance Act No. 4 of 1988 repealed section 27 of the Income Tax Act which required a married woman's income to be assessed together with that of her husband for the purpose of income tax.

Again in Zimbabwe, the Deceased Persons Family Maintenance Act, 1987, established the right of the surviving spouse to continue to occupy the matrimonial home and use the household goods and effects as immediately before the death of the spouse or parent and enjoy the crops and animals as they did before. Interference with these rights was made a criminal offence. Moreover, the Equal Pay Regulations, 1980, corrected the discriminatory practice where women doing the same work as men received less wages. Under these new regulations, men and women now receive the same rates of wages for similar work, at least in law.

In Uganda, the Administrator General's Act makes it an offence to interfere in the property of a deceased person without the authority of court or the Administrator General. However the enforcement of these laws is again hampered by unsatisfactory application. For example, the High Court has made the letter of no objection from husband's relatives a mandatory requirement before a widow is granted letters of administration. Also the police have been reluctant to enforce the law against the relatives of the deceased who grab property. Both are contrary to the spirit and the letter of the law, but are practised by law enforcement institutions (OkumuWengi 1994).

Likewise Namibia's Married Persons Equality Act No. 1 of 1996 has put to an end the age old marital authority of the husband to deal with family property alone. The Act is still rather new and it remains to be seen how it will work out in practice.

In Eritrea the Land Proclamation of 1994 provides that every adult of 18 years and above is entitled to obtain land. This proclamation also allows women to obtain land for housing in their villages of origin. Thus in principle this proclamation recognises equal rights to land for both men and women, irrespective of marital status.

These examples show that positive gains have been registered in the area of women's legal status in a number of Southern and Eastern African countries, and notably in those which have emerged from protracted liberation struggles.

The Tanzanian context

This part of the paper will focus on Tanzania's capacity building and utilisation of human resources, particularly those of women through legislative and policy measures.

Tanzania has been in the forefront in fighting for freedom in other countries, equitable distribution of resources between citizens and nations and to some extent between the sexes. Moreover, it was among the first African countries to introduce affirmative action such as women's representation in the Party and in Parliament, quotas in education as well as the ground breaking LMA in 1971.

Rural poverty in Tanzania has been said to be caused by weak economic production and consequently the difficulty of extracting an adequate surplus from a harsh agricultural environment. Studies and fact finding missions conducted recently around the country have concluded that, among other things, cultural and traditional practices which are outdated have negative impacts on the status of women and children and society in general (Ministry of Community Development Women Affairs and Children, 1994). Other findings show that an asymmetrical division of labour results in women being constantly tired from working long hours. Patriarchal power relations were identified which put ownership, control and management of resources in the hands of men while women are the main producers, accounting for over 75 per cent of food production. The domineering nature of some males within a patriarchal system was also found to contribute to "women's lack of incentives to work hard". All these findings reflect on women's weak legal status. They illustrate women's lack of bargaining power at household level to induce men to share in the production burdens. Often domestic violence is used to force women's compliance. However, women's lack of choices to opt out of an oppressive system of production is an underlying factor.

The legal framework for the women of Tanzania as regards eradication/alleviation of poverty among women can be analysed through the constitution, family laws and property laws. The Constitution of Tanzania permits discrimination on the basis of sex. However, Article 24 recognises every person's right to own property and this includes women. As for property laws, the most significant for women remain inheritance and property rights during marriage and divorce.

Inheritance laws

There are three regimes of succession and inheritance laws including customary, Islamic Laws and Statutory Laws. The Law applicable to most African women is Customary and Islamic Law. According to Customary Law a daughter can only inherit in the third degree if there are no sons or if the son(s) are dead, and they did not leave male offspring. Even when a daughter inherits she cannot pass on the inherited immovable property to her own children because they would invariably belong to a clan other than her own. Conversely, this does not apply to their brothers, because children are affiliated and therefore belong to their fathers' clans in patrilineal societies which constitute 80 per cent of the country's ethnic identities. Before court intervention in 1990 women heirs were not allowed to sell inherited land. In practice lack of rights results in labour constraints for women and has implications for their old age security.

Women spend most of their productive lives in marriage and it is there they have the best opportunity to invest. Paradoxically, the Customary Law regime does not give widows any inheritance rights in their own right. Instead it gives a widow three choices, to go back to her own people, to live with her children where they had been allocated to live or finally, to be inherited by a relative of the deceased and live together with him as husband and wife under the leverage custom of widow inheritance.

All these options are problematic in practice and modern day thinking. For one, the widow may not have a natal home after many years of marriage. Two, if the widow's children with the deceased are not males, they have a small to no share of the land.

Likewise non-first born sons and non-last born sons in some ethnic communities such as the Chagga do not present much hope for the widow either. To derive maximum benefit from this law, a widow has to be senior or only wife, and has to have at least one son—endowed with a good conscience so that he will look after his mother. Moreover, if the widow's children with the deceased are daughters, then she would be left empty handed (Rwebangira, 1996).

A study I conducted in 1995 on the legal status of women and poverty in Tanzania revealed four main findings. One, was that despite women's contribution in the family, their labour is expropriated through marriage and inheritance laws, coupled with the practice of law enforcing institutions such as courts and clans that discriminate against women and hand over the fruits of their labour to men. It was argued that this in practice denied women a creative role to empower themselves economically. Moreover, the discrimination also discourages many women from taking initiatives on their own behalf as they remain uncertain of the extent to which their interests in the fruits of their labour and investment are protected. The uncertainty comes from the experience of daily witnessing the humiliation suffered by divorced and widowed women due to weak legal protection of their rights. As most Tanzanian women (98.4 per cent) spend a significant part of their productive lives in marriage, such uncertainty and apprehension can only stifle married women's desire to give the best of themselves in the family and community. In such a situation how can Tanzania fight poverty?

Another finding showed that despite Tanzania's record of promoting equality, equity between nations and egalitarian principles since independence, very few laws promoting women's rights and especially economic rights have actually been enacted in the last twenty years. Of the 351 new laws that were enacted between 1975 and 1995, only 8 had gender based implications. These new laws included the Village and Ujamaa Village Act (Registration, Designation and Administration (Villagization), Act No. 21 of 1975; the 5th Constitutional Amendment Act of 1984; the Penal Code, Employment Ordinance (as amended by Act No. 91 of 1975); the Education Act of 1978; the Day Care Centre Act, No. 17 of 1981; Ratification of CEDAW in 1985 (technically not a law as it is not automatically enforceable in domestic courts); the Cooperative Societies Act, 1991; and the Regulation of Land Tenure (Established Villages) Act No. 22 of 1992.

Even among these eight laws only the Education Act, 1978 and the amendment to Cooperative Societies Act, 1991 had sufficient focus on the impact on women's poverty. Moreover, they were not backed by structural and institutional, policy and legal changes sufficient to alleviate women's poverty. This related to women's lack of ownership and control of land and the contraction of social services which meant drastic cuts in spending on education, resulting in slow expansion for secondary education, lack of jobs etc., thereby dampening the education momentum.

The third finding of the study was that women's economic rights are not a government priority. This finding was derived from the fact that reforms likely to enhance women's economic position such as the Law of Succession and raising the minimum of age of marriage for girls from 14 to 18 years were not acted upon by government. The Law of Succession, in particular, has stalled far too long and successive governments have shelved it indefinitely since 1968, although Kenya and Uganda have put such legislation in place. It is amazing that Tanzania, being economically the poorest of the three countries, finds it politically sensitive and is perhaps unsure of the macro economic benefits of motivating its most readily available investors, women, in the mainstay of the economy, agriculture.

The fourth and final finding was that although there was a large number of NGOs dealing with gender and women's rights in the country, the constituency of women was weak politically and therefore not taken seriously by party leaders and election candidates. I suggested in the study that capacity building skills in the context of human rights, lobbying and advocacy were essential for civil society. The skills required include strategies gaining legitimacy in women's communities while at the same time encouraging women to think and act politically on the basis of their own interests.

In conclusion I disputed Tanzanians relatively good policies on gender equity as very little has been done in practice that could reduce or alleviate poverty among women. In spite of the external forces that may be contributing to our poverty, we can make a difference if we harness all our internal resources and move together as a community by applying some home made remedies. One such remedy is to give women a stake in the prospering of their families, community and nation at large and hence encourage them to think beyond subsistence. Such confidence can only flow from a firm legal status backed by serious institutional support to implement the relevant policies.

The recommendations for change to reverse the trend include:

– Expansion of legal services for women so as to encourage women to claim their existing legal rights and force decisions to be made on strategic aspects that continue to hinder women's exit from the cycle of poverty.

– Effective use of the media to communicate much needed information so as to empower women and youth especially to participate confidently in the affairs of their community from village to national and even international levels.

– Targeting specific desired legal changes.

– Effective collaboration and co-ordination of efforts between government, NGOs and institutions working on gender equity.

Summary and conclusion

This paper has attempted to show that the inferior legal status of women contributes to development of poverty among women. This is done on two levels: women are denied tools with which to assert themselves in their communities and in inter-personal relations, and the resultant insecurity disconnects women from a vision of prosperity beyond subsistence.

Policy makers and development agents have for a long time grappled with integrating women into "development", in reality meaning into production in order to increase the volume of goods and services. Not, however, for the benefit of women, but rather this was seen to be a duty to their families, communities and nations. Does this sound familiar? We have heard it before and it did not work. Why would it work for African economies? We are not only talking of equitable distribution of resources as a human right here. We are also talking of motivating the worker in order to enhance production and well-being.

References

Economic Commission for Africa (1998): "Strategies for enhancing favourable legal environment to promote women's access to productive resources within the family framework", Africa Centre for Women. Paper presented at the ECA/CONESA High Level Seminar on Gender Equity, Social and Economic Empowerment of Women held in Lusaka, Zambia, 6–9 April, 1998.

Economic Commission for Africa (no date): COMESA High Level Seminar on Gender Equity, Social and Economic Empowerment of Women. Draft Report, Lusaka, Zambia.

Gopal, B. & Salim (eds.) (1998): *Gender and Law: Eastern Africa Speaks*. The World Bank, The Economic Commission for Africa. Proceedings of a Regional Conference in Addis Ababa, Ethiopia in Oct. 1997) IBRD, Washington, DC.

Gachukia, E. (1991): Comment at the Annual Conference of the International Women's Rights Action Watch (IWRAW), Roosevelt Hotel, January 1991, New York, USA.

Havnevik, K.J., (1995): "Pressing Land Tenure Issues in Tanzania in the Light of Experiences from Other Sub-Saharan African Countries". *Forum for Development Studies*. No. 2, 1995. Norwegian Institute for International Affairs, Oslo, pp 267–284.

Makombe, I.A.M. et al., (1997): "Credit Schemes and Women's Empowerment for Poverty Alleviation: The Case of Tanga Region". A Preliminary Research Report submitted to REPOA Secretariat, Dar es Salaam.

Mbughuni P., (1994): *Gender and Poverty Alleviation in Tanzania: Issues from and for Research*. REPOA Special Report, Dar es Salaam University Press, Dar es Salaam.

Ministry of Community Development, Women Affairs and Children (1994): Women and Poverty Alleviation in Mara Region. Seminar held at Musoma 14–17 September, 1994, Dar es Salaam.

Rwebangira, M. (1996): *The Legal Status of Women and Poverty in Tanzania*. Research Report No. 100, The Nordic Africa Institute, Uppsala.

Chapter 8
Practising Partnership for Poverty Eradication: Dilemmas, Trade-offs and Sequences

David Booth

Introduction

Current thinking about world poverty is increasingly influenced by two (relatively) new ideas: 1) that poverty is not just about economics but involves power and "voice"; and 2) that international assistance for poverty-reduction should be based on new forms of partnership. This paper argues that although in principle these policy concepts reinforce each other, human and institutional resource constraints are such that a partnership-based approach to poverty reduction involves difficult operational choices. It is worth distinguishing simple dilemmas, trade-offs of various types and more or less difficult sequencing issues. These choices are increasingly recognised; it is time to start talking about them and accumulating relevant experience.

> Some 1.3 billion people … continue to live in extreme poverty, on less than the equivalent of $1 per day …. They lack access to opportunities and services …. They feel isolated and powerless and often feel excluded by ethnicity, caste, geography, gender or disability …. They believe nobody listens, and often have no way of being heard in places where the decisions which affect their lives are made (UK, 1997, 10).

> Poverty, like wealth, is not a clear-cut or easily defined concept. Its causes and characteristics differ between and within countries and regions, as well as between different social groups …. (When) poor people describe their own poverty or that of other people … often the picture they present differs from the conventional picture, which equates poverty with a lack of material resources. Their definitions are more holistic, diverse, multidimensional, cross-sectoral and culture-specific. They also relate to a lack of access to and control over social, economic and political resources (Sweden, 1997, 10).

> Fighting poverty within the framework of development cooperation involves direct action to alleviate suffering, but the principal objective is to help the poor to rid themselves of poverty by their own efforts. The main responsibility lies with the individual countries. Their will and capacity to pursue a policy of combating poverty are crucial. ….. There is currently widespread agreement among donors that partnerships must be established instead of the traditional donor-recipient relationship (Sweden, 1997, 8, 57).

Until donor assistance systematically goes through the budget and utilises core public sector systems and structures, the way we provide aid will be part of the problem rather than part of the solution (Foster and Merotto, 1997, 2–3).

How then to ensure that sector-wide approaches to health development address the needs of the poor and help to reduce poverty? In posing this question, it is important to recognise that it reflects a growing suspicion in some quarters that SWAps are inherently 'statist', centralising, top-down, solely concerned with upstream policy issues and the supply of services, rather than mechanisms that help the poor articulate demand for better health care (Cassels, 1997, 26).

There is no a priori reason why a sector-wide approach should lead to greater central control, and the establishment of decentralised systems needs to be a key component of the collaborative programme of work (Cassels, 1997, 28).

Background

For good reason, the closing years of the twentieth century are being marked by a ferment of ideas about more effective means of addressing the challenge of world poverty. Two ideas in particular have made substantial headway in the course of the 1990s. Together, they promise to make a substantial difference to the way the task of poverty reduction is tackled during the next decades.

One the one hand, along with general adoption of the headline targets for poverty reduction set in 1996 by the OECD Development Assistance Committee (DAC), there is growing recognition that *poverty and its reduction are not just economic issues*.

What matters to poor people about their poverty has more than one dimension. The capital assets that are important in pulling people out of poverty are more varied than previously suspected, and include the quality of the social and political relationships in which they find themselves embedded. Above all, reducing poverty may have less to do with technicalities than with restoring power and "voice" to the poor, or with radically altering the conceptual and political frameworks of those who are in a position to influence the allocation of resources. Though not yet universally recognised (and, to be frank, still subject to rather crude formulations), these statements, or something like them, are close to becoming the mainstream view in several bilateral development agencies.

On the other hand is the revolution in thinking about donor-recipient-beneficiary relationships implied by *new concepts of partnership*. This takes various forms: at the macro level, the spread of flexible programme funding through recipient-government budgets; at sector level, sector investment programmes (SIPs) and, more particularly, sector-wide approaches (SWAps) based on pooled effort under recipient-government co-ordination within an agreed framework.

What is common to these formulations is recognition that uncoordinated donor spending outside the frameworks of national and sectoral budgets is an inefficient and counter-productive way of addressing the challenge of the DAC targets—increasingly, indeed, part of the problem rather than part of the solution. The new partnership approaches promise both greater governmental ownership of development plans and a means of advancing donor priorities that is more effective than the coercive conditionalities of the recent past. For these reasons, ideas about partnership are increasingly favoured and prominent in the strategic statements of leading development agencies.

The problem

When two ideas come into their own simultaneously, as has happened here, it is very much to be hoped that they are consistent and capable of mutually-reinforcing application. Were they to be in conflict in any significant respect, it would be important to know this well in advance, so as not to build up expectations that may be disappointed, possibly prompting disillusionment with the whole project of raising resources for a final assault on world poverty.

At one level, there is no problem. As current policy statements insist, there are strong reasons why better partnerships should be considered preconditions for more effective poverty reduction, and vice versa.

On the one side, without the broader reviews of total expenditure and the inclusive sector plans promised by the partnership approach, we cannot even guess what the aggregate impact of our efforts towards poverty reduction currently is, let alone make sensible judgements about how things might be improved. If we cannot account effectively for inputs (expenditure), how can we expect to make sound judgements about desirable changes in outputs (services), let alone about the processes that lead from outputs to the outcomes that figure in the DAC targets?

In reverse, if the partnerships are not partnerships *for* poverty reduction, they will simply not be entered into, given donors' strategic commitments. Donor strategies increasingly visualise a two-pronged approach. Where developing-country governments disqualify themselves as potential partners by blatant neglect of the economic and other rights of poor people, more localised, less official and more direct forms of partnership with poor people or intermediary organisations will be pursued instead. Thus, it is said, the pursuit of partnership will never be an obstacle to helping the poor.

This is convincing enough at the very aggregate level at which such statements are made. At this level, there is no questioning the mutuality between greater effectiveness in approaching poverty and greater sophistication in managing aid. This paper stands by the overall good sense of a partnership approach to poverty-reduction efforts.

I do, however, want to suggest a short pause for reflection, and then a longer-term commitment to monitoring practice and learning quickly on the basis of experience in applying the approach. For although there may be no fundamental conflict between partnership and poverty-reduction, except in the case of a few rogue regimes, the real world is unfortunately not as tidy or as simple as our general policy statements suggest.

In particular:

Developing-country governments do not fall neatly into two categories, those that are worthy partners, and those that are not. Although it is clear enough why some regimes may be considered beyond the pale, the assumption that the rest are in some equally simple sense within it, is obviously unrealistic. In the real world, it is typically the case that policy commitments run well ahead of actual results; vary in seriousness both across and within major sectors of activity; and remain in crucial ways untested. There are solid reasons why this should normally be the case.

Though the technical preconditions of transparency and accountability which are emphasised in partnership-oriented approaches are also preconditions for carrying through commitments to poverty-reduction targets, they are not the only preconditions. Herein lies a fundamental problem. For it is not only conceivable but observable in particular cases that achievements in these different terms do not always match each other, and even, sometimes, move in different directions.

The argument

These things being the case, this paper argues, there is a need to learn more about ways of handling the tensions and managing the choices involved in practising partnership for poverty reduction. In particular, we need to distinguish more clearly between:

– irreconcilable conflicts or dilemmas;

– trade-offs, of either the zero-sum or other varieties;

– sequencing problems, calling for different trade-offs at different stages in a *process*;

– conflicts between different forms of partnership that may conceal choices of one or more of the above types.

The argument of the paper is shamelessly exploratory. It is based loosely on some recent country enquiries undertaken on behalf of UK DFID and Sida in Africa and, to a lesser extent, Latin America, together with some ongoing rethinking about the policy relevance of different approaches to poverty analysis. The propositions advanced are certainly no more than working hypotheses.

The main point is to test out the degree to which they may be shared by others, as agenda items for further discussion.[1]

The need for social and political realism

Why is it suggested that developing partnerships that are serious about poverty reduction may be difficult, even in what are normally considered acceptable partner countries? Answering this question involves no new thinking, but merely recalling elements of what (following the World Summit on Social Development) may now be considered accepted wisdom.

The balance of international and national influences and peer pressures works strongly in favour of verbal commitments to shared objectives on poverty reduction, combined with policies-in-practice that reflect, voluntarily or otherwise, the ideas and interests of the non-poor.

"All power deceives", as Robert Chambers (1997) would say. Policies-in-practice reflect professional ideologies that privilege top-down applications of knowledge over the perceptions and grasp of relevant information of poor people. They also tend to be informed by a "rationalist" view of the policy process, in which what counts is the formulation of a sound plan, the rest being considered a mere problem of implementation. This encourages a systematic downgrading of enquiries into outputs and outcomes, or into the realities of policy on the ground.

For both of the above reasons, achieving poverty-focused national or sectoral planning involves a challenge to the cosy technicality of accustomed forms of policy dialogue between donors and recipients; it involves "speaking truth to power" in ways that neither set of participants may find easy. Though the capacity of developing-country policy makers to rise to this challenge is not at all to be underestimated, the likelihood of whole sectors embarking simultaneously on such a change, at all levels, seems small.

None of this is in any way new or surprising. It clashes to some extent with the warm rhetoric of partnership, but that is not the point. The important thing is to try to move on and spell out the operational implications of these common observations.

The central point of what follows is to distinguish between several ways of viewing the potential conflicts between partnership and poverty-focus, and on this basis to suggest ways in which we might hone our ideas about managing them, in partnership or otherwise.

---

[1] These lines were written just ahead of the publication of Norton and Bird's excellent (1998) paper, which both reflects several of the same concerns and fills out the agenda suggested here in a practical and imaginative way.

Dilemmas, trade-offs and sequences

Dilemmas

The first point to establish is that in general there is *not* a basis for viewing the partnership/poverty-focus issue as an irreconcilable conflict or pure dilemma. There are certainly some tendencies in current thinking and practice that might push us towards such a conclusion, but the argument of this paper is that they should be rejected.

For example, Robert Chambers' persistent suggestion (ibid.) that the viewpoints of poor people and those of most policy makers belong to different "paradigms" (or incompatible sets of master-concepts) would logically imply that partnerships, other than direct partnerships with poor people's organisations, stand a poor chance of being poverty-reducing. Or, to change the metaphor somewhat, if the question is "whose reality counts?", the answer is surely not the sort of compromise and persuasion in the context of shared assumptions that is at the heart of flexible funding and SWAps.

The division of labour between different types of professional advisers in some agencies—in which certain professionals take a special interest in top-down accountability, while others have a special brief for assessing outcomes from the bottom up—may lend some apparent validity to this sort of dualistic vision. However, I believe that it is both problematic as social science and contradicted by everyday practice. There are not two realities but constructed structures (Berry, 1993; Gould, 1997) that are not fully grasped by anybody, especially in the absence of dialogue, iteration, triangulation. If that seems obscure, the essential point is simple: dialogue and learning can and do take place across the supposed gulf between so-called paradigms. So poverty-reducing partnership is not a contradiction in terms.

Trade-offs

The above implies that in general there is no obligation to choose *either* partnership *or* poverty-focused intervention. However, it does not follow from this that there are no difficult choices to be made.

The key problem is that achieving success in a partnership approach, with poverty reduction as the central objective, is generally recognised to be very intensive in human and organisational resources. Donor funding is certainly not the main constraint. The main constraint is the political commitment, organisational drive and collective personal effort that are required of the institution that is the central focus under a partnership approach, the finance ministry or sectoral or district authorities of the implementing government.

Can a major effort be sustained on improving management information systems and financial accountability (a precondition for flexible funding in all cases) without any cost in terms of the required attention to quality of service delivery and evaluation of outcomes? Since the latter also calls for a major and unaccustomed effort, the answer would seem to be certainly not.

That is to say, there certainly *is* a trade-off. The only question that might be debated in a particular case is whether this is a simple zero-sum relationship, or something rather less stark. Does the concentration on systems that, say, a health SWAp implies lead to an equal and opposite effect on the capacity to monitor and do something about health standards on the ground? Or is it just that it is not possible to make substantial advances on both fronts at the same time? And, in either case, on what basis should the choice be made?

Sequences

It seems likely that the way development agencies and their partners answer such questions will be influenced by implicit or explicit views of the expected *sequences*. However, it is already clear that different agency advisers take opposing views on this issue, both of which appear at first sight to make good sense.

On the one hand, there is the "first things first" approach: first get your budgeting systems and expenditure monitoring in place, so that donor resources can be pooled and a dialogue begun on the basis of solid data, full transparency and mutual respect. Then the difficult, non-obvious question of how spending might be better directed to contribute to poverty reduction can be tackled with some confidence that the information can be handled, and in a way that guarantees national scope and sustained results. It might be added that the reformist zeal that is required to achieve the first thing is a scarce, wasting resource which must be focused when it is available to achieve the necessary breakthrough and not dissipated by taking on too many tasks simultaneously.

Opposing this is the view that, in this matter as in life in general, it is better to start off the way you intend to continue. Given political realities, professional ideologies and all the other things we now understand about the nature of poverty-producing social environments, we can have no confidence that if attention to quality of service, poor people's access to services and actual outcomes, is not on the policy agenda from the outset, it will ever get onto it in the future.

There is a serious danger, in other words, that the enthusiasm for flexible funding arrangements and SWAps, in which recipient interest in ownership is strongly reinforced by donor interest in accountability, will exhaust all the available reformist energy before what is really fundamental—effectively targeted outputs—can be tackled. Rather like the strategic sequence implied in the old 1960s concept of "high growth plus trickle-down", the initial priorities may set up obstacles to the later benefits' ever being realised.

This is, of course, on the arguably over-optimistic assumption that a flexible-funding or sector-wide approach is genuinely capable of delivering the necessary co-ordination and confidence in a particular case. The worries that arise about trading-off attention to the poverty focus of outputs and outcomes against allegedly more fundamental management reforms are serious even when the latter have some real chance of success. The concern must be even greater if they do not.

Current observations in a number of countries suggest that under the influence of new partnership ideas and responding to pressures to commit more funds to what can be presented as poverty-related sectors, some donors may be seriously over-stretching the absorptive capacity of sectoral ministries (e.g. OPM, 1997). Weak SIPS or SWAps may deliver neither kind of desired result.

I do not suggest that these difficulties are anyone's fault, or that those presently grappling with them are unconscious of their implications. The point is to emphasise that they are general problems, not those of one country or sector; that they are quite fundamental, not mere matters of implementation; and that they are not going to go away. They need to be discussed more widely than they presently are.

The Issue of decentralisation

A final example concerns a stronger version of the sequencing problem just alluded to. Is it possible that the success of a SWAp, in management-of-funding terms, might not just leave a sector reform programme too exhausted to take on further change, but also set up political obstacles to such change?

Take administrative and financial decentralisation, widely regarded as a precondition for forms of planning that come closer to meeting the real needs of poor people. In Cassels' sanguine formulation, quoted among the epigraphs to this paper, there is no inherent contradiction between SWAps and decentralised systems. Thus, decentralisation should definitely be part of the collaborative work programme. One might add that in the well-known case of the Zambian health SWAp, the process may be said to have been led by decentralisation, negotiations over the common district funding basket having preceded by several years those over any pooling of effort at the national level.

This, however, misses the main point. There may well be a benign relationship between SWAps and decentralised planning when decentralisation is conceived in sector-wise terms. But it is certainly not conceived in this way by everybody. There is a widely-held view that the key to meeting the needs of poor people and attaining the DAC targets is to persuade governments to undertake a comprehensive devolution of public expenditure to levels of administration where the voice and influence of the poor majority can be felt.

The obstacles to actually achieving this are many and substantial. However, the success of sector-wise decentralisation, particularly if it has been undertaken completely without reference to elected local authorities, can and does set up fresh obstacles to radical decentralisation, in the form of a new set of stakeholders with an interest in the status quo.

This might be considered as a conflict between two possible styles of partnership, one focused on line ministries, the other on local governments with multi-sectoral responsibilities. However, in most countries central ministries are much better placed to develop strong relationships with donors than local governments are. That could be regarded as a major sense in which vigorous pursuit of a sector-wide approach by donors could seriously set back the chances of instituting forms of planning that take the needs of the poor as their starting point. The potential for a conflict of this type has been noted by some observers of the health-sector reforms in both Zambia and Ghana.

This too is an issue on which there are and will continue to be different views. I do not suggest that it should be considered settled. On the contrary, I propose that the choices that are implied need to be discussed and evaluated in a more explicit and wide-ranging way.

Conclusion

This paper has scratched the surface of a number of issues. It may also have bitten off more than it can chew. It will, however, have served its purpose if it suggests the need for more explicit reflection on the trade-offs and sequences that are entailed by a simultaneous commitment to ambitious poverty-reduction objectives and more satisfactory forms of partnership between donors and recipient governments. There is not yet a great deal of experience to go on, and what has been drawn on in the paper has been used implicitly and with some hesitation. What this suggests is the need for openness to fresh learning and the diffusion of good practice on the operational practicalities of reconciling two worthwhile but difficult objectives.

References

Berry, Sara (1993): *No Condition is Permanent: The Social Dynamics of Agrarian Change in Sub-Saharan Africa*, Madison: University of Wisconsin Press.

Cassels, Andrew (1997): *A Guide to Sector-Wide Approaches for Health Development: Concepts, Issues and Working Arrangements*, Geneva: WHO, DANIDA, DFID, EC.

Chambers, Robert (1997): Whose Reality Counts? Putting the First Last, London: Intermediate Technology Publications.

Foster, Mick and Dino Merotto (1997): "Partnership for Development in Africa: A Framework for Flexible Funding", London: UK Department for International Development, Africa Economics Department, mimeo.

Gould, Jeremy (1997): *Localizing Modernity: Action, Interest and Association in Rural Zambia*, Helsinki: Finnish Anthropological Society.

Norton, Andrew and Bella Bird (1998): "Social Development Issues in Sector Wide Approaches", London: UK Department for International Development, Social Development Division, Working Paper 1, May.

Oxford Policy Management (1997): "Sector Investment Programmes in Africa: Issues and Experience", Oxford: OPM, January.

Sweden (1997): *The Rights of the Poor—Our Common Responsibility* (Government Report 1996/97, 169), Stockholm: Ministry for Foreign Affairs.

UK (1997): *Eliminating World Poverty: A Challenge for the 21st Century* (White Paper on International Development), London: The Stationery Office.

List of Participants

Ms. Dorrit Alopaeus-Ståhl
Minister
Permanent Representative to FAO,
WFP and IFAD
Embassy of Sweden, Rome

Mr. Fawzi Al-Sultan
President
International Fund for Agricultural
Development

Ms. Abla Benhammouche
Country Portfolio Manager
International Fund for Agricultural
Development

Prof. David Booth
Centre for Development Studies
University of Wales

Dr. Vigdis Broch Due
Senior Research Fellow
The Nordic Africa Institute, Uppsala

Ms. Elisabet Brolin
Administrative Officer
Division for International
Development Cooperation
Swedish Ministry for Foreign Affairs

Mr. Lennart Båge
Head of Division
Division for International
Development Cooperation
Swedish Ministry for Foreign Affairs

Prof. Andrew Dragun
Department of Economics
Swedish University of Agricultural
Sciences

Mr. Jan Cedergren
Director General
International Development
Cooperation and Migration
Swedish Ministry for Foreign Affairs

Ms. Gloria Davis
Director

Social Development Department
The World Bank

Mr. Dag Ehrenpreis
Head of Economic and Social
Analysis Division

Division for Policy and Corporate
Development
Swedish International Development
Cooperation Agency, Sida

Mr. Karl Johan Fogelström
Managing Director
Swedish Cooperative Centre

Mr. Steinar Hagen
Deputy Director
Technical Department
Norwegian Agency for Development
Cooperation

Prof. Kjell Havnevik
Department of Rural Development
Studies
Swedish University of Agricultural
Sciences

Mr. Peter Herthelius,
Programme Coordinator
Department for Natural Resources
and the Environment
Swedish International Development
Cooperation Agency

Mr. Johan Holmberg
Director
Department for Natural Resources
and the Environment
Swedish International Development
Cooperation Agency

Mr. Gary Howe
Acting Director
East and Southern Africa Division
International Fund for Agricultural
Development

Mr. Mats Hårsmar
Secretary of Study and Research
Swedish Mission Council

Mr. Bo Jerlström
Deputy Head
Division for International
Development Cooperation
Swedish Ministry for Foreign Affairs

Ms. Ritva Jolkkonen
Deputy Director General
Division for Multilateral
Development Issues
Finnish Ministry for Foreign Affairs

Ms. Gerd Johnsson
Counsellor
Division for Global Cooperation
Swedish Ministry for Foreign Affairs

Ms. Pernilla Josefsson
Senior Administrative Officer
Division for International
Development Cooperation
Swedish Ministry for Foreign Affairs

Mr. Mats Karlsson
State Secretary
Swedish Ministry for Foreign Affairs

Ms. Fröydis Kvalöy
Senior Executive Officer
Noragric
Agricultural University of Norway

Mr. Prosper Matondi
Research Fellow
Department of Rural Development
Studies
Swedish University of Agricultural
Sciences

Dr. Thandika Mkandawire
Director
United Nation Research Institute for
Social Development

Mr. Taysir Mustafa
Media Relations Coordinator
International Fund for Agricultural
Development

Dr. Abdul Raufu Mustapha
Queen Elisabeth House
University of Oxford

Mr. Ole Mölgard-Andersen
Chief Adviser
Danish Ministry for Foreign Affairs

Dr. Tekeste Negash
Consultant on Development and
Educational Issues in Africa

Mr. Per-Ulf Nilsson
Programme Officer
Department for Africa
Swedish International Development
Cooperation Agency

Ms. Gunilla Olsson
Special Policy Adviser
Division for International
Development Cooperation
Swedish Ministry for Foreign Affairs

Dr. Adebayo Olukoshi
Senior Research Fellow
The Nordic Africa Institute, Uppsala

Mr. Atiqur Rahman
Lead Strategist and Policy
Coordinator
Economic Policy and Resource
Strategy Department
International Fund for Agricultural
Development

Ms. Magdalena Rwebangira
Lawyer
High Court of Tanzania

Dr. Oliver Saasa
Director
Institute of Economic and Social
Research
University of Zambia

Mr. Emil Sandström
Seminar Coordinator
Department of Rural Development
Studies
Swedish University of Agricultural
Sciences

Dr. Pekka Seppälä
Research Fellow
Institute of Development Studies
University of Helsinki

Mr. Arild Skåra
Senior Adviser
Technical Department
Norwegian Agency for International
Development Cooperation

Dr. Michael Ståhl
Director
Council for Development and
Assistance Studies
University of Uppsala

Ms. Ann-Margret Sveidqvist
Secretary
Department of Rural Development
Studies
Swedish University of Agricultural
Sciences

Ms. Lotta Sylwander
Social Development Adviser
Swedish International Development
Cooperation Agency
Embassy of Sweden, Pretoria

Ms. Daphne Tuvesson
Editor
Forests, Trees and People Newsletter
Department of Rural Development
Studies
Swedish University of Agricultural
Sciences

Mr. Lennart Wohlgemuth
Director
The Nordic Africa Institute, Uppsala

Dr. Prudence Woodford-Berger
Lecturer, Department of Social
Anthropology
Development Studies Unit
Stockholm University

Mr. Håkan Åkesson
Deputy Director
Division for Africa
Swedish Ministry for Foreign Affairs